Portfolio of
Low-Expense Art Lessons:
Featuring
43 Novel Display Techniques

Anne Martin

Portfolio of Low-Expense Art Lessons: Featuring 43 Novel Display Techniques

Parker Publishing Company, Inc. West Nyack, N.Y.

© 1977, by

PARKER PUBLISHING COMPANY, INC.
West Nyack, New York

All rights reserved. No part of this book
may be reproduced in any form or by any
means, without permission in writing
from the publisher.

Library of Congress Cataloging in Publication Data

Martin, Anne,
    Portfolio of low expense art lessons.

    Includes index.
    1. Art--Study and teaching (Elementary)--United States. 2. Project method of teaching. 3. Displays in education. I. Title.
N362.M37   372.5'044   76-44007
ISBN 0-13-686469-4

Printed in the United States of America

Introduction

Elementary teachers are frequently in need of art lessons which are not only interesting and satisfying to their classes but which result in exhibitable art products. The projects in this book are planned so that individual skills are both challenged and developed and directions are given so that the products can be integrated to create unusual displays. These are much enjoyed when viewed by students, administrators, teachers, and parents.

The projects use low expense and scrap materials which are readily available in all schools, and the procedures for lessons and displays are structured to promote easy understanding and presentation. There are unlimited opportunities for individual expression, and when techniques are thoroughly understood the over-all plans can be custom fitted to class and teacher.

That artistic skill exists in varying degrees cannot be denied. However, *all* the work from these projects can be displayed effectively. Some students' products might exhibit less artistic merit than others but will exude a great deal of appeal if the display is done carefully using the techniques described at the end of each lesson. An unattractive display could detract from the individual child's work, and therefore the display techniques become almost as important as the projects themselves.

Successful displays make a positive contribution toward the child's attitude-formation. His self-confidence is enhanced and he is proud to identify with his class and his school because he has helped to make it more attractive.

All the ideas in PORTFOLIO OF LOW EXPENSE ART LESSONS: *Featuring 43 Novel Display Techniques* have been successfully classroom-tested, and the photographed results are entirely the work of students at the Covington Elementary School in Oak Lawn, Illinois. It is our hope that students and teachers everywhere may derive the same kind of rewarding satisfactions from these lessons as we have experienced.

Anne Martin

Before Beginning the Lessons

1. Have the children make the various component parts of these displays, but plan to put the displays up yourself. If you leave the displays to them, or foist the job off on a "bulletin board committee," they'll take three weeks to do what you can do in fifteen minutes.
2. A display does not have to be assembled on a bulletin board. If you don't have one on your room (or in the hall), use the wall itself and stick the display parts to it with circles of masking tape.
3. Encourage your students to bring in any usable material being discarded at home. (e.g., carpet remnants, leftover wallpaper, plastic packing pieces, fabric, etc.) Never refuse *anything*. (You can always slip it into a shopping bag and take it home to stow it in your garbage can if it's *really* unusable.) But keep up a receptive front, and eventually you'll get some real treasures.
4. Start some organized collections of paper in Scrap Boxes. You will need three boxes, so that the children can quickly and easily find the colors they are looking for: 1) *Warm Colors* (red, yellow, orange, brown), 2) *Cool Colors* (green blue, purple), 3) *Neutrals* (black, white, gray). This is handy for teaching color classifications and saves a lot of paper which might otherwise be thrown away.

Contents

Chapter 1 UNUSUAL ANIMALS 17

    Lesson 1   Stuffed Paper Fish   19
    Lesson 2   Alley Cats   23
    Lesson 3   Cows and Trees   26
    Lesson 4   Carousel Horses   32
    Lesson 5   Comical Birds in Cages   36
    Lesson 6   Calm Clams at the Beach   42

Chapter 2 ANIMALS IN UNUSUAL SETTINGS 49

    Lesson 1   Alligators in Daffodil Land   50
    Lesson 2   Cabbages and Kangaroos   54
    Lesson 3   Mice and Clocks   58
    Lesson 4   Pear in a Partridge Tree   63
    Lesson 5   Donkeys and Dandelions   67

Chapter 3 HOUSES FOR LOOKING INTO 71

    Lesson 1   Life in a Medieval Castle   72
    Lesson 2   See-Into Victorian Houses   77
    Lesson 3   Giant Beehive   80
    Lesson 4   Life Aboard a U.F.O.   83
    Lesson 5   Henhouse   87

Chapter 4 PICTURES IN VARIED SHAPES 91

    Lesson 1   Paintings on Real Leaves   92
    Lesson 2   Raindrops   95
    Lesson 3   Star Worlds   98
    Lesson 4   Lift-Up-Object Paintings   101
    Lesson 5   Paintings in a Basket   105

Chapter 5   **TEXTURED SEMI-3-D ANIMALS**..............109

     Lesson 1   Shaggy Carpet-Scrap Lions   110
     Lesson 2   Fabric and Paper Turtles   114
     Lesson 3   Plastic-Packing-Pieces Rabbits   118
     Lesson 4   Toothpick Porcupines   122
     Lesson 5   Rope Camels   126
     Lesson 6   Cone Creatures   131
     Lesson 7   Caterpillars & Co.   136

Chapter 6   **PAPER AND CRAYON MURALS**..............141

     Lesson 1   Lions and Palm Tree   142
     Lesson 2   City Cats   146
     Lesson 3   Elves and Mushrooms in Moonlight   151
     Lesson 4   Little Foxes and Chickens   156
     Lesson 5   Seahorses and Octopuses   161
     Lesson 6   Sit-Down People   167

Chapter 7   **DYNAMIC FIGURES**..............171

     Lesson 1   Running and Jumping Scarecrows   172
     Lesson 2   Raincoated Puddle-Jumpers   177
     Lesson 3   Elves at Work   181
     Lesson 4   Balloonists in Berry Baskets   187
     Lesson 5   Walnut-Head People   193
     Lesson 6   Humpty-Dumpties   197
     Lesson 7   Sailors on a Yacht   201
     Lesson 8   Dancing Skeletons   205
     Lesson 9   Silhouettes Go to a Picnic   209

Index 217

Portfolio of
Low-Expense Art Lessons:
Featuring
43 Novel Display Techniques

Chapter 1. Unusual Animals

Lesson 1
Stuffed Paper Fish

Stuffed Paper Fish

The beauty of this project lies in its simplicity, as well as in the eye appeal of the finished results. Children love it, and it literally cleans up by itself because the fish "eat" all the paper scraps that would usually be picked up and thrown into the waste basket.

Preparation

All you need is two sheets of bright-colored 12" × 18" construction paper for each child, and a volley ball net (borrowed from the gym teacher).

Presentation

Pass out one of the sheets of the 12" × 18" paper to each of the children and tell them to place the paper horizontally across their desks.

On the board, show how they should put a dot in the middle of both the long edges of the paper:

and then another dot halfway up the left side. Give each dot a number:

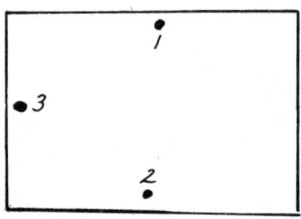

Now draw a curved line from #3 up to #1 and then down to the lower right-hand corner:

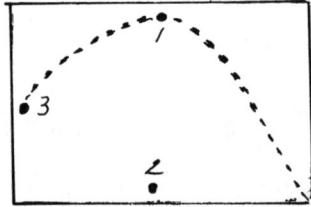

Repeat the process, but this time go from #3 down to #2 and then up to the *upper* right hand corner:

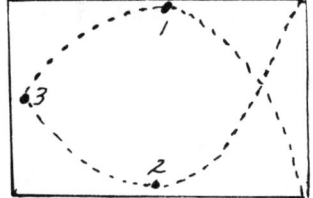

The students will then recognize the beginning of a fish form. (If mistakes occur, they should be corrected by erasing and trying again and *not* by turning the paper over and starting again on the back.)

Give the tail more of a fish-like appearance by rounding it off, and also widen it where it joins the body by adding some more lines:

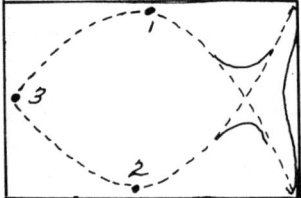

Pass out a second sheet of the 12″ × 18″ paper to the children and instruct them to stack it directly underneath the first.

Holding both sheets tightly together, cut out the fish outline. Be careful not to cut the tail off. When the cutting has been finished keep the two fish together and put an X on the stomach.

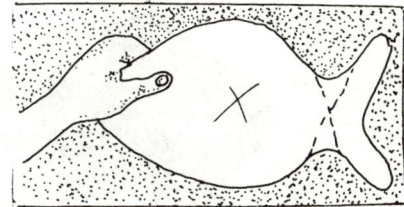

Then (still holding them together) flop them over and put an X on the stomach of the other fish:

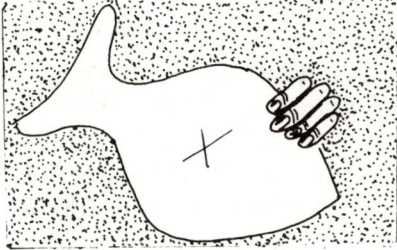

Separate the fish and place them across the desk with noses touching and both X'd sides exposed:

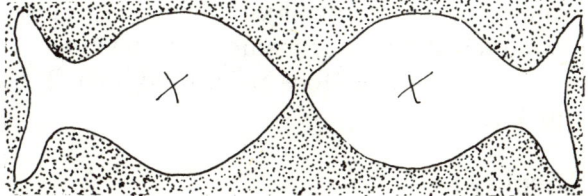

(The reason for the X's is to insure a matched fit when they are put back together again.)

Apply glue all the way around the edges of one of the fish, as close to the edge as possible.

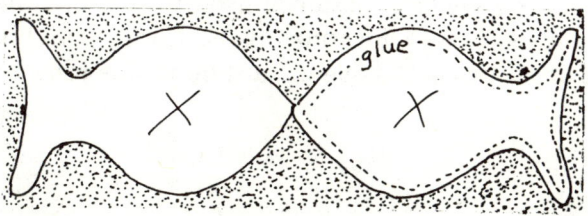

Then put the two fish together so that the X's are on the inside.

Break up the space with pencil lines and add some design and patterning. Put in a line for the mouth and add an eye. For example:

Unusual Animals

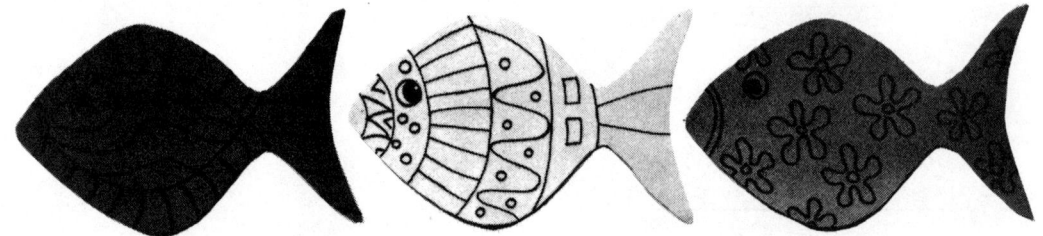

Turn the fish over and design the other side. The designs may be the same, or they may be completely different, since only one side of the fish can be viewed at a time.

If available, black markers can be used to go over the pencil lines to finalize the design and give it a more finished look. The designs can be either colored in with crayon or painted in, but painting will take considerably longer. Also, the color of the construction paper can be allowed to show for some areas of the design.

When the coloring has been completed, clip the mouth off and force it open with a ruler. Crumple up bits of the scraps left over from the cutting-out phase of the project and "feed" the fish. Poke the paper all the way inside with the ruler, but do it gently to avoid tearing. If tearing does occur (and it *will*), have a stapler handy for quick repair.

Display

Hang your volley ball net either on a wall or from the middle of the ceiling. Hook the fish to the net with pulled out paper clips:

An added touch for this display is plastic "bubbles." These are made from plastic packing material used to prevent the breakage of fragile items such as Christmas balls. Construction paper "fish hooks" and dried grass "seaweed" are good finishing touches too.

Lesson 2
Alley Cats

Alley Cats

Preparation

Cut out of construction paper some pointy shapes that resemble picket fences.

Your colors may be mixed or monochromatic. Also, cut out some garbage cans and lids

and finish with tempera or crayon lines. You will need a large yellow moon too.

Presentation

Pass out sheets of 12" × 18" (white) drawing paper to your class, and help them to pencil in some large cat drawings. On the

Unusual Animals

chalk board, you can give them a few starting helps, such as faces viewed from the front

or from the side

and feline body construction:

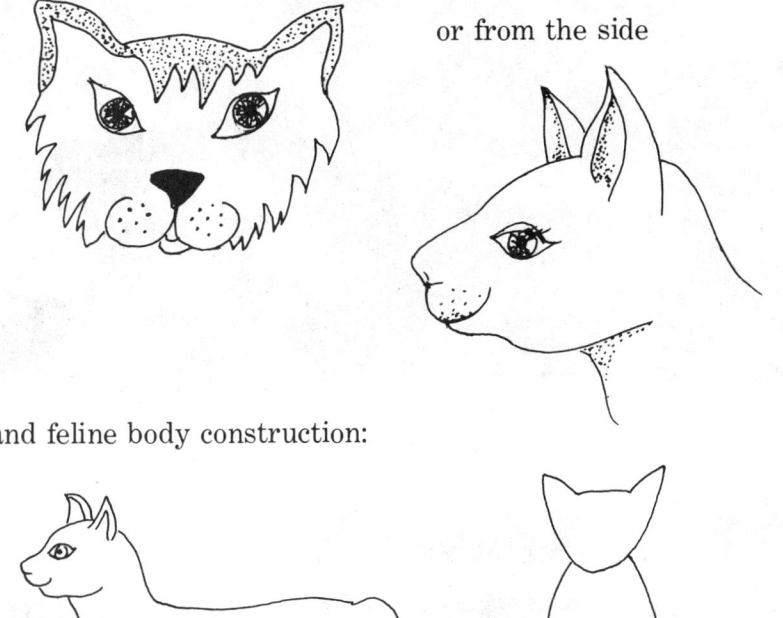

Discuss what the cats are up to in a back alley late at night. Show the class the fences, moon and garbage cans, and tell them to make their cats to fit the setting.

When drawings are complete, set out tempera paints. Black, white, brown, yellow, green and red are essential, but any additional colors will be welcome.

None of the cats should be cut out until the painting phase is completed and the pictures are dry.

Display

Arrange background and cats harmoniously on the bulletin board. Let your sense of humor guide you.

Unusual Animals

Lesson 3
Cows and Trees

Cows and Trees

This project is a simple lesson in crayon drawing which is quite, restful, and satisfying. It is surprisingly successful with primary-grade children.

Preparation

Light brown construction paper works best for drawing cows; the 9″ ×12″ size, is large enough.

The trees can be done on 12″ × 18″ light green or yellow paper.

Presentation

Children are usually eager to draw a cow without any help at all, but for those who seem at a loss to know where to begin, a suggestion as to how to draw the head may be welcome.

Start with an oval nose in the middle of the left side of the paper:

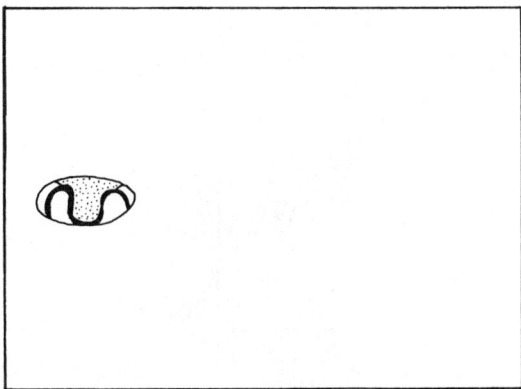

Unusual Animals

The rest of the drawing of the head is developed from the nose and should allow plenty of room for the body:

Drawing the body should be left entirely to the student; the individual interpretations will be very diverse and interesting. After the drawing is completed, the cows can be colored entirely with crayon or left with much of the brown paper color showing. Be cautious in cutting: you might need to have a roll of tape handy to mend ears and tails.

After the paper for the trees has been passed out, tell the children to get out a light brown crayon and a dark brown crayon. Begin the drawing with the lighter shade and make the shape of a capital Y:

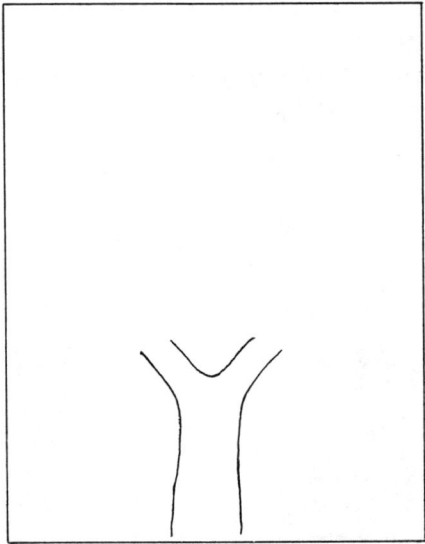

Then let each fork of the Y become the stem of another Y.

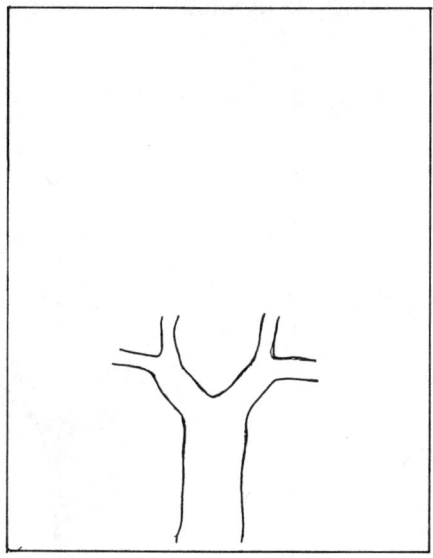

Color the left side of trunk and limbs light brown and the right sides of each with dark brown. Let the colors overlap in the middle so that you get a shaded effect which makes the limbs look rounded.

Using a pencil, sketch in some puffy leaf sections. Explain to the students that it is not necessary to draw individual leaves, but that they should be shown in clusters.

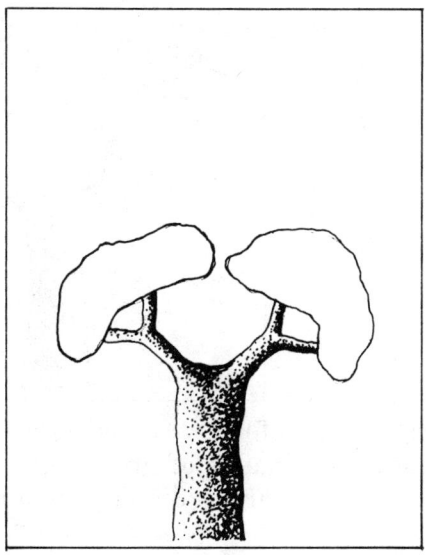

Unusual Animals

Now add more Ys on top of each cluster and more clusters on top of each Y, making them smaller as you go higher.

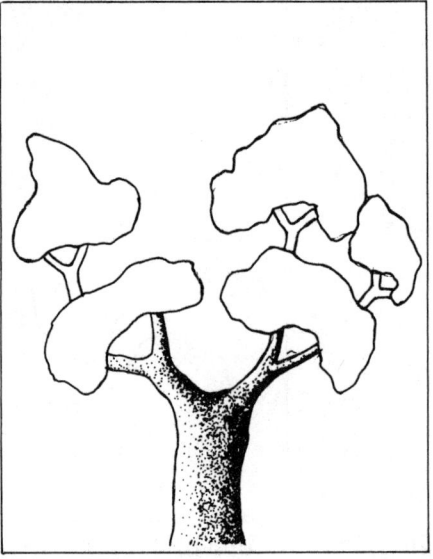

Join all the clusters with wiggly lines and round off the entire foliage area in the process.

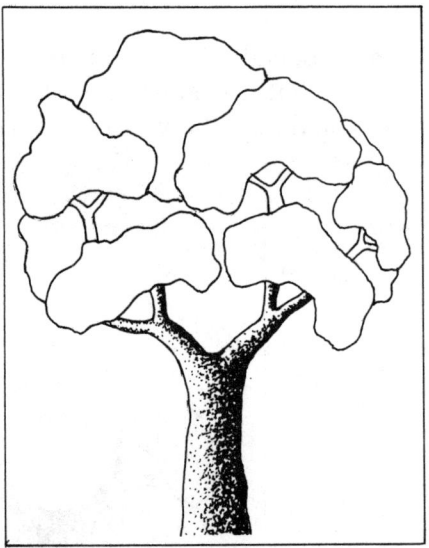

Color in all the limbs as before with the light and dark brown crayons. Then select two shades of green. Begin with the dark green, and color in all the areas directly behind the limbs and branches.

All the rest of the leaf clusters will be light green, since they are catching more light.

Additional shades of green, if available, may be blended into the drawing for further textural and color variation. The overall application should be waxy and will have the effect of an oil painting.

Display

Cut some rounded hills from as many different shades of green construction paper as you can find. Overlap some, as you put them up, and create an area large enough to accommodate all of the trees and cows.

Scatter the small trees in the background and place the larger ones in the foreground. The large ones will perhaps need to overlap.

The cows bask under the trees on the hills and again should be placed according to size.

Break up a plastic berry basket and tape up the sections to make a fence. Popsicle sticks could be used for a fancier fence, but it will take a lot longer to put it up.

Lesson 4
Carousel Horses

Carousel Horses

Preparation

Practice drawing a horse when you're alone. Block it in first with ovals and rectangles:

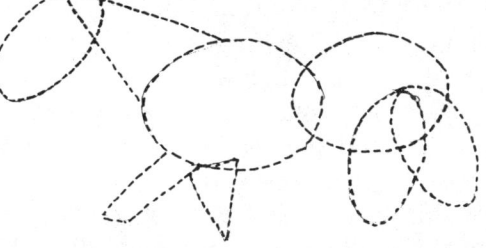

The front legs bend twice (at the knees and the hooves). The back legs are drawn from oval and triangular shapes. Add the fleshy details around the geometric block outline, plus ears, tail and mane:

If you feel confident enough after your private practicing session, then present this drawing sequence to your class on the chalkboard. Do one step at a time while they follow you. If, however, you feel timid about using this direct approach, put the drawing on the board the night before or at some other time when the class is out of the room. You could also draw it on a large piece of newsprint paper if you cannot sacrifice the chalkboard space.

Presentation

Let each child choose a piece of 12" × 19" construction paper from a variety of colors. The drawing should progress slowly and carefully. Having drawn the horse yourself, you will be aware of the areas of difficulty and be more able to guide your students.

After the rough pencil drawings are completed, start the conversion process from *real* horse to *carousel* horse. This operation will give some children new confidence. If anyone has judged his drawing to be "unreal," he can now proceed to turn those shortcomings into advantages as he converts his "horse" into a facsimile painted wooden horse.

Set out your paints, scrap paper box and shiny colored foil scraps. Help the students to recall all their memories of carousel horses: they are carved from wood and brightly painted; their eyes are shiny; they have extravagantly decorated bridles and saddles; the reins are sometimes embellished in the manner of medieval knights' horses' reins; they look as though they are galloping, but are low enough for a child to climb upon.

The horses may be painted or left in the color of the construction paper. Accessories may be fashioned from colored scrap paper and then decorated with shiny foil and/or painted. A bit of glitter here and there (if you've managed to save some) works well in this project.

Display

Cut a 1" × 18" strip of yellow construction paper for each horse and stripe it diagonally with gold crayon (or with glitter if you're rich!) Tape one to each horse to simulate the metal mounting post.

Tape a long line of 6" × 18" orange paper to a wall (one strip for each horse you plan to put up) to simulate a carousel base. Now put up the horses, grounding the posts in the base in such a way that all the horses are relatively uniform in height.

To suggest the umbrella-like top of the carousel (and to conceal the tops of the mounting posts), cut a set of scalloped sections from two contrasting colors of construction paper. Start by chopping up 9" × 12" sheets into three twelve-inch lengths per sheet. Round off one end of each of these 3" × 12" segments and then fold back the remaining square ends one inch.

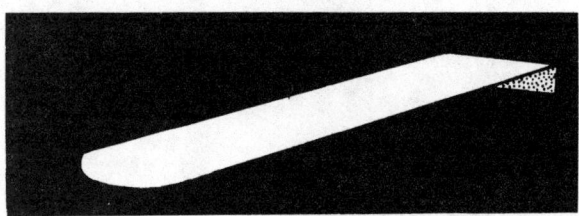

You will need six of these umbrella scallops for each horse you plan to put up. Put circles of masking tape on the back of the folded edges, and stick them to the wall above the horses. The tensile strength of the paper at the fold will hold it out just enough above the horses to create a semi-3-D canopy effect. The colors of the scallops should be alternated.

Unusual Animals

Lesson 5
Comical Birds in Cages

Comical Birds in Cages

Preparation

Hang up a paper birdcage on its fancy chain at the front of your classroom. You will, of course, have to make it first; here's how:

Start with a piece of 6" × 9" colored construction paper and cut it in half so that you have two 3" × 9" pieces. Lay one piece on top of the other and fold them in the middle. Keeping the pieces together, cut a wavy line along the bottom edge, working from the fold on out toward the end. Curve the cutting line up when you reach the end.

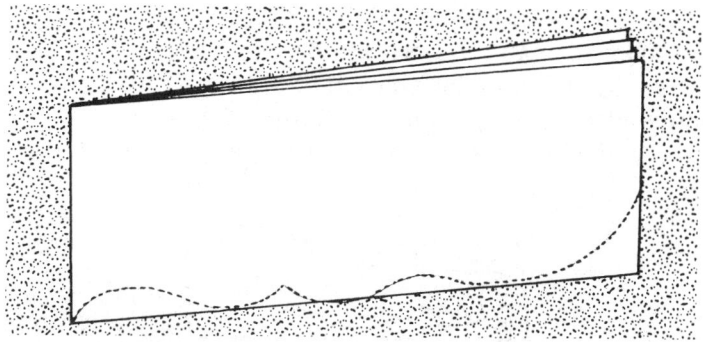

Unfold the pieces and lay them on a sheet of 9" × 12" black construction paper so that the wavy edges point away from each other. There should be an inch of the top and the bottom of the black paper concealed by these colored pieces; it will then begin to look like a birdcage:

Cut five 1/4" × 12" strips of colored paper for the bars. Put a dab of glue on each end of one of these bars, and attach the ends at the middle of the top and bottom cage-sections (easily located by the fold lines, which will still be showing). Leave the cage sections in the same position on the black paper while you are gluing the bars in place. This will prevent the problem of lopsidedness. Glue two bars to the extreme right and left sides of the cage and then the last two can be easily positioned in the remaining spaces. Turn the cage over so that the bars are on the back.

Cut a ring of paper for the top of the cage and attach it. Make some symmetrical decorations by folding a piece of 3" × 9" paper (any color which contrasts to that of the cage) and cutting several random elongated forms:

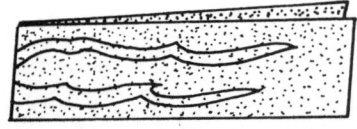

Unfold the decorations and match the fold lines to those on the cage sections for easy centering. Put one on the top and one at the bottom. Cut some more, if you want to be elaborate, from fluorescent or foil papers.

Now glue the cage to the black paper: apply the glue to the back of the top cage section and press it down even with the top of the black paper. Then glue on the bottom in such a way as to force the bars to protrude outward for a semi-3-D effect.

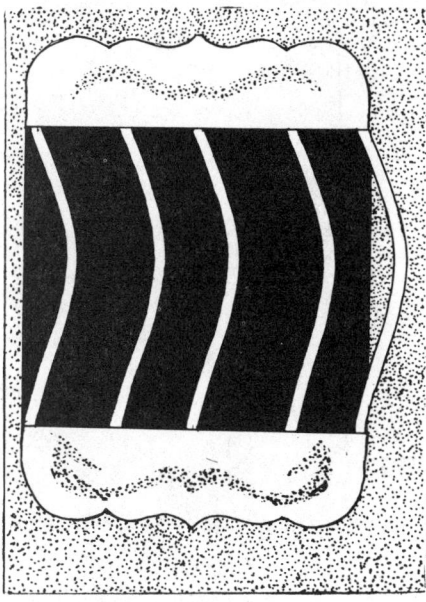

Make a fancy chain to attach to the cage: cut a 2″ × 18″ strip of paper and fold, first crosswise and then lengthwise. Cut a series of scallops along the free edge; then cut the centers out of the scallops from the folded edge:

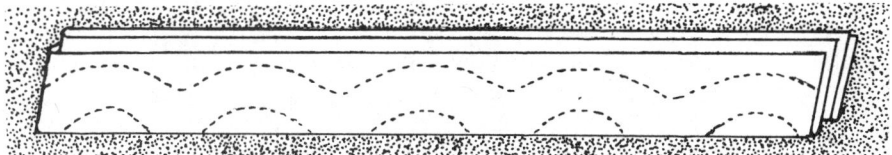

Unfold the resulting "chain" and glue it to a 2″ × 18″ strip of black paper; then attach it to your cage.

Presentation

Put up your cage on the wall and invite the children to discuss what kind of bird would live in such a different cage. Set about making the birds by chopping some 9″ × 12″ assorted colored paper in half and letting each child choose two 6″ × 9″ pieces of contrasting colors. Lay one piece on top of the other and fold in half the long way. Draw half an oval on the lower part of the paper and cut out so that you have matching shapes but different colors.

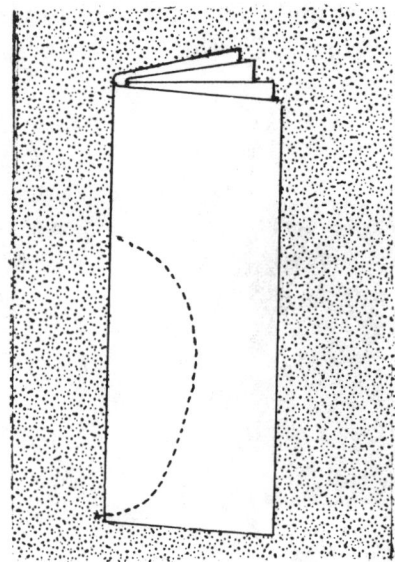

Refold one of the ovals and cut it into feathered wings.

Lay the wings on the body and experiment with their placement:

Attach with glue when ready.

Cut head and tail from the remaining paper. Keep it folded if you want symmetry, or work with it unfolded for free forms.

After the heads and tails are in place, the children can decide what color to make the beaks and feet, and then get that paper from the scrap box. Shapes of feet may vary from rounded to clawed. Beaks may be semi-three-dimensional or flat.

Everyone will need a small piece of black and white paper for eyes. Circles of white may be glued to larger circles of black or the other way around.

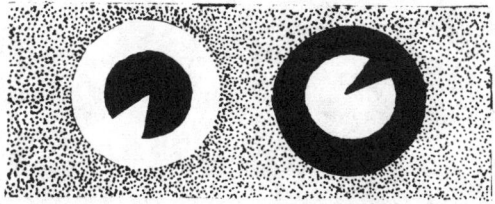

Before the eyes are glued to the bird's head, experiment with their placement. A cross-eyed effect is always amusing to children, and it might be suggested to them if they do not happen to discover it themselves.

Real feathers add a nice finishing touch to these birds. Lacking feathers, try unraveling string, rope, or yarn, and perch it on top of the head. Sequins, buttons, or colored candy lifesavers make interesting additions to the eyes. (N.B.: If you decide on the lifesavers, be sure to have plenty of extras.)

Make the cages and place the birds in them before the final gluing to be sure that heads and feet are not going to be concealed by the cage sections.

Chains may be made, as suggested earlier, or they may be varied by using square or triangular cuts instead of scallops. Old-fashioned link paper chains (the Christmas tree variety) are also very effective if made with very small links of black paper.

Display

Tape the bird cage to a wall in a random fashion. Add to some of the chain lengths so that all the cages appear to be hanging either from the ceiling or from another cage.

Lesson 6
Calm Clams at the Beach

Calm Clams

Preparation

Start saving eggshell halves well in advance of the day you plan to present this project. You will need one half-shell for each student, plus some extras to compensate for mistakes.

Some children might not be familiar with the fact that mollusks, such as clams, consist not only of an outer shell but of bodies as well. It should be made clear to them that clam bodies are in reality very soft and the shells hard.

It might even be possible for you to bring in two or three real fresh-water clams and keep them alive in a sandy-bottomed fish tank for several days while the children observe. (This might provide a welcome change from the old fish and turtle lessons.)

At any rate, the students are going to make three-dimensional *pictures* of clams, and they will bear only a passing resemblance to real ones.

Presentation

Black construction paper will be needed for the clam shells, and the 6″ × 9″ size will be about right. Put a drawing of the shell shape on the chalkboard and tell the students to fold their paper and draw the shape using a white crayon. The shape need not be exact. Anything from a "rounded" triangle to a circle will work. Keep the paper folded during cutting so that two matching forms are produced. After they are cut out, but still being held in the hand, put a little X on the inside of each shell so that they can easily be matched later.

Get out white and grey crayons, plus silver, if you have them. The top shell is going to be colored with these crayons in such a way as to represent the texture of the clam shell in a decorative way. Begin with a heavily applied line of white that goes all the way around the outer edge. Next use the grey and then the silver. Demonstrate on the chalkboard the routes these lines are to take. Continue alternating crayons until the shell has been entirely colored. Some of the black paper may show between the lines; this will emphasize the pattern.

Tell the students to place the two shells back together with the X inside. Go around the room with the stapler and make a little staple tuck at the hinge end of each of the shells, making the top one (the one that's been crayoned) bulge out and the bottom one bulge in.

Pass out 2″ × 4″ rectangles of yellow construction paper and have each child write his name. Poke a paper fastener through the two clam shells (from the inside) and on through the yellow paper, making sure the child's name is on the back:

Unusual Animals

The yellow paper serves not only to identify the artist but to provide a means of applying tape to the clams for display later.

Pass an eggshell half to each child along with drawing ink and pens (if available) or fine-tip black markers.

Each child should draw a face very carefully on the egg shell. These will, of course, turn out to be somewhat anthropomorphic caricatures of clams, but anything goes! After the faces are drawn, some color can be added with water colors. Provide a very small brush to be used in this operation; caution should be taken to use as little water as possible.

When the faces are dry they can be either taped or rubber cemented to the inside of the clam shells.

Beach umbrellas make a nice complement to this display. (Some students could be working on umbrellas while they are wait-

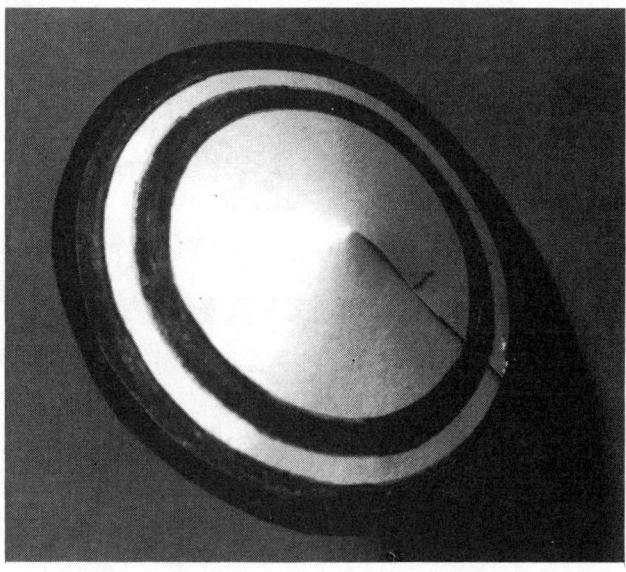

ing their turns for water colors or ink in the clam part of the project.) Have available some circles of yellow and orange paper. They should range in sizes from four inches to six inches in diameter. When designs have been outlined in pencil they should be heavily and neatly colored in crayon. (Warm colors are most effective.) Glue the umbrellas to black paper and cut out, leaving 1/4" black edging all around. Cut in toward the center and overlap slightly to get the umbrella to point out, and then fasten the overlap with glue or a staple.

Display

Cut some low sand dunes from peach-colored paper. You will need about eleven of them. For a more interesting textural effect, make the dunes from sheets of sandpaper. (Cutting through sandpaper will also sharpen all of your scissors—but you knew that!)

Take four sheets of 9" × 12" yellow paper and make some zig-zag cuts across it at one-inch intervals:

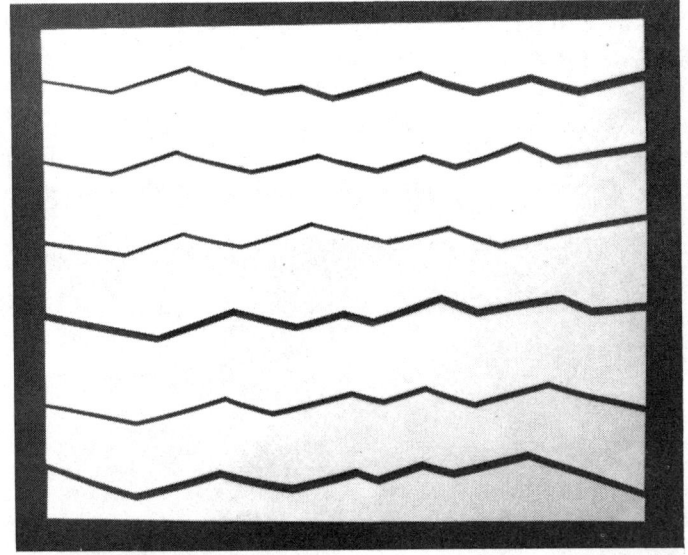

Staple eight sheets of dark blue into 9" high cylinders.

Cut some 4" high waves from light blue and some 2" high ones from turquoise. Glue wisps of cotton to the waves' crests.

Now select your display wall, assemble all your pieces and get out your masking tape.

Begin with the umbrellas at a point slightly below your own

eye level. Tape them in a random row across the wall. In front of them and in between, place the sand dunes so that they overlap here and there.

Start a row of the yellow-zig-zags just below the dunes and add clams in groups between them. (These yellow zig-zags represent the water marks which are left on a beach each time a wave retreats. They should be allowed to bulge out here and there for greater emphasis of line.)

After all the clams have been incorporated into the shore line (they should end up at child's eye level), put up the ocean. Tape up the eight dark blue cylinders in a straight line across the bottom of the display. Glue or tape a row of light-blue waves on to the cylinders and let flashes of dark blue show in between. The short, turquoise waves go on last and can be interspersed among the others.

Chapter 2. Animals in Unusual Settings

Lesson 1
Alligators in Daffodil Land

Alligators in Daffodil Land

Preparation

Get a yellow dixie cup for each child—or get some small white paper cups from the school nurse and have the children paint them yellow, and allow to dry. Cut a 6" × 6" square of yellow construction paper for each child and a 3" × 18" rectangle of spring green. This will take care of the daffodil materials.

To make the alligators, use green rubber carpet padding scraps—the kind that resembles a waffle. Ask your class to help you locate some of this. (N.B.: They might bring in the jute kind of carpet padding by mistake, but hang on to that—you can use it for other projects later in the year.) Try to collect enough of this material so that each child can have a piece about 12" × 3". They will also need a 6" × 2" piece of dark green construction paper (for legs and feet), white and black paper (for eyes), a bit of colored yarn for a whimsical neck bow, and a tiny square of pink fabric for a tongue.

Presentation

Pass out all the alligator materials first and show this simple shape on the chalkboard.

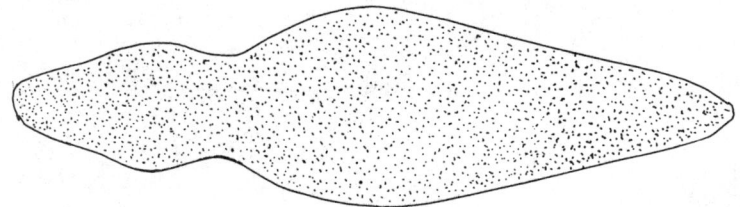

Animals in Unusual Settings

The shape should be cut out directly without preliminary drawing. Tell the children to let the tail become as long as the rubber allows.

Legs and feet can be drawn first and then cut from the folded dark green paper,

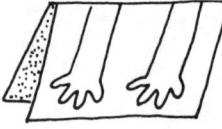

then glued to the underside of the alligator.

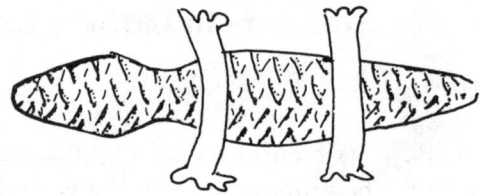

Cut out white ovals for eyes and small black circles for their centers, and glue *all* these in place. Add bow and tongue and set the creatures aside to dry.

Daffodils

After materials are distributed, instruct each child to place his cup in the center of the yellow paper and draw a circle around it.

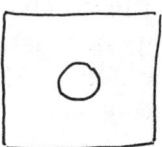

After removing the cup, draw a line directly through the circle.

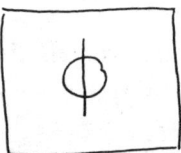

Divide the left half with two lines

52   **Animals in Unusual Settings**

and then also divide the right half with two lines:

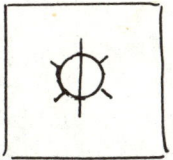

Now draw the flower petals using the lines as a guide for equal distribution.

Cut out the flower and glue the cup in place.
Add stem and leaves cut from the spring green paper.

Display

Cut some free-form cloud shapes from sky blue paper

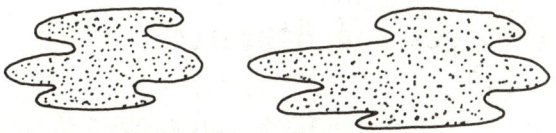

and some similar water shapes from dark blue paper.

Arrange on the bulletin board with the flowers jutting well into the sky and the alligators swimming happily in the "water" beneath.

Lesson 2
Cabbages and Kangaroos

Cabbages and Kangaroos

Kangaroos are appealing to children both by themselves and as a drawing subject. These animal drawings combined with cabbage forms make a provocative display.

Preparation

Each student should have a 9" × 12" piece of grey construction paper and a half sheet of white. Some small scraps of pink can be passed out later for the inside of the ears.

Presentation

Some children will be able to draw a kangaroo without any help, but the ones who need it will feel more confident if you put a simple drawing on the board. Point out the pear-shape of the head

and use that as a starting point. Children like to exaggerate the size of the tail and feet, so additional grey paper may be needed by some of them.

After the grey form is finished, cut it out and place it over the sheet of white so that the front part of the animal may be drawn from chin to pouch.

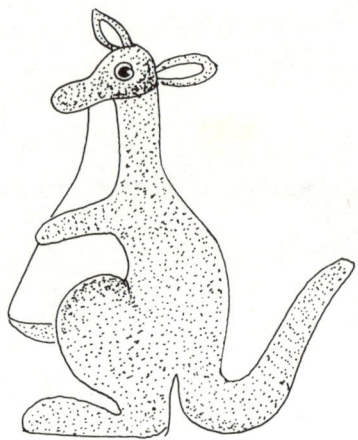

Using a ticket-punch, give each child a black circle and show all how to cut a tiny wedge out for a shiny eye. The cleft circle can then be glued to a scrap of white paper and cut out so that white surrounds the black dot. Glue the eye in place and pass out pink paper for the inside of the ear. They are made to fit by tracing the shape of the grey ears and then cutting a slightly smaller pink shape so that there will be grey showing all around. Do one ear at a time so that the children won't get the shapes mixed up.

After the kangaroos are completed and everyone has had enough fun teaching them to hop around the desk tops, you are ready to tackle the cabbages. Pass out 9" × 12" white drawing paper (the cheaper the better) and tell everyone to find a light green crayon. Each one will be able to draw two or three cabbage leaf shapes on the paper using the crayon. This should be heavily applied so that the lines are nicely waxy. Meanwhile, dilute some green tempera (one to one) with water. This solution, painted over the crayon outline, produces an interesting wax resist effect. Allow these to dry overnight.

Next day, the cabbage leaves should be cut out and stapled together (with a little folded tuck at the base) for a semi-3-D effect. If your students are not quite able to manage this, perhaps you

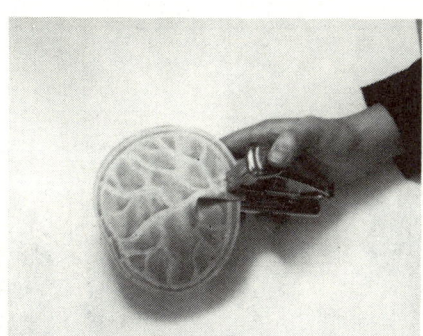

could enlist the help of a student aide—or do it yourself at the lunch table.

Display

Cut six or eight rolling hills from black construction paper. Put them up in an overlapping line on the wall. Place a nice big orange sun in back of them (this is a good place to print your room number and the display title). Sort out the kangaroos and cabbages into three piles according to size. Put up the smallest ones in the back right against the hills so that the black contrasts nicely with the color of the animals. Alternate the cabbages with the kangaroos and continue until all are included in the display. You might find it interesting to group several of the cabbage leaves into overlapped heads of various sizes. Red cabbages could be produced just as easily, by simply changing crayon and paint color.

Animals in Unusual Settings

Lesson 3
Mice and Clocks

Hickory Dickory Dock

This lesson could be combined with an arithmetic unit on telling time and/or learning to write Roman numerals. The clocks should be made first;

Preparation

Find some pictures of antique clocks. (Catalog photos of antique clock reproductions will do nicely if your local library has nothing to offer on real antiques.) Make the pictures available to the children and point out both the decorative features and the practical ones. (Of course it would be absolutely great if you could bring in a real antique and demonstrate pendulum action, weight function, and the striking mechanism.)

Presentation

Pass out 9″ × 12″ white drawing paper and a half sheet of black. The clock faces should be cut from the white. They may be either round or square, but should be kept large enough so that the children are not cramped for space when it's time to put on the numerals. Instruct them to divide the clock faces with pencil dots using the old method; then fill in the remaining digits in between.

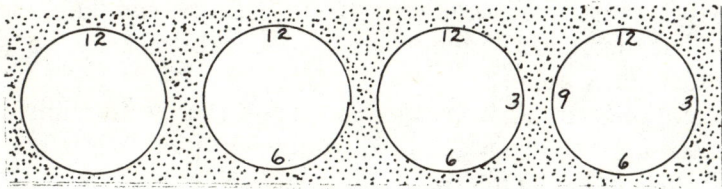

Next they should draw in the numbers (or Roman numerals) with pencil and then trace over the pencil lines with black marker. The hands of the clock should be made of black paper and may be plain or fancy. If available, cellophane (clear or colored) could be used to simulate glass.

Make an assortment of 12″ × 18″ paper available and let each child choose one sheet to make the housing for his clock face. After it has been determined how wide the housing must be in order to accommodate the size of the face, one side of the case is drawn in pencil and the paper folded in half. Cut with paper folded to achieve symmetry.

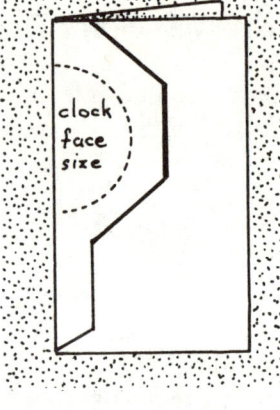

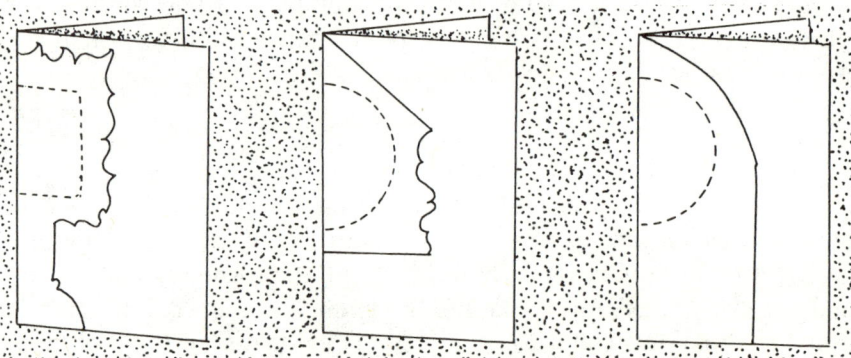

After gluing the clock face on to its case, a pendulum, weights, doors, cuckoos, and "gingerbread" decorations may be added, using scrap box paper.

Mice, to go in between the clocks and to give the finished display more appeal, are assembled from grey, pink, white and black paper. Pass to each child 6″ × 9″ grey, 3″ × 2″ pink, 3″ × 2″ white and 3″ × 2″ black pieces. Begin with the pink paper and draw the inner ears:

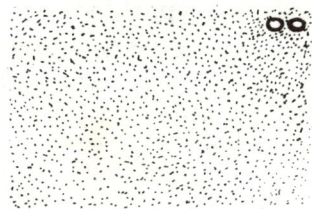

Cut out and then glue these two pink circles to the grey paper:

Then cut them out again, this time leaving a margin of the grey showing around the pink. Put the ears aside to await assembly; then, continuing to work with the remaining grey paper, make the head, body, legs and tail.

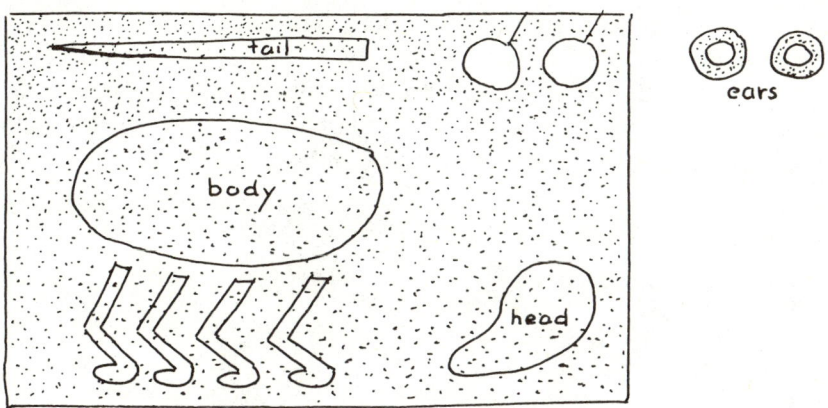

Point out that the legs should be bent to get the look of action. The length of the tail should be left to the child; you may expect some outrageously long ones.

 Cut a small circle from the black and remove a small wedge. Glue this to the white paper and cut out again:

This is the eye; only one will be needed since the figure is being shown in profile.

Animals in Unusual Settings

Cut out the rest of the parts and assemble:

One or both of the ears may be used, leaving this decision to the individual child. The legs should be tried in several different positions before gluing, and the addition of noses, shoes, collars and bows should be encouraged.

Display

Put up the clocks first in a random but balanced arrangement. The larger ones should be somewhat higher and the smaller ones can overlap them slightly and be hung lower.

String yarn in a criss-cross random way from clock to clock, diagonally, and then put up the mice. This is the fun part. They can be chasing each other, posing on top of several clocks or even in some. You will know which arrangement will amuse your children most. You might also want to include the "Hickory Dickory Dock" nursery rhyme somewhere in the display.

Lesson 4
Pear in a Partridge Tree

A Pear in a Partridge Tree

The "tree" in this display is made up entirely of feathers (green if possible) and partridges. A lone pear is nested cozily on one of the top branches. All who see it have fun figuring out what it must be.

Preparation

Buy some small (2 or 3-inch) white feathers at a craft supply store. You will need at least two for each of your students when they make the birds. Also you will need a dozen large green feathers to construct the tree. (If they don't have them at the craft store, try the toy section of the dime store, or look for "Indian hats.") You will also need about four tubes of silver glitter.

Presentation

Pass out one 9" × 12" sheet of construction paper to each child. Have the paper folded the short way and put a few suggested simplified bird shapes on the board.

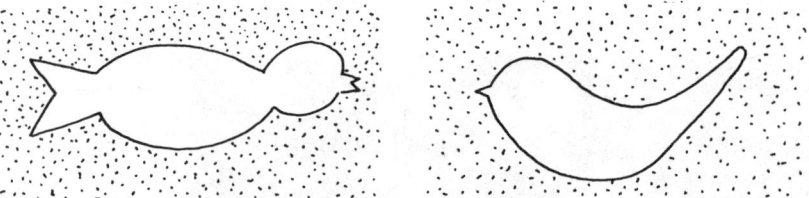

Also give some suggestions as to simplified designs within the bird shapes:

After designs are penciled in, they should be painted with tempera in two or three colors (at most).

When the paint is dry, the birds can be cut out, keeping the paper folded so as to get two thicknesses.

Pass out the small white feathers (two or three to each child), and as the painted front of the bird is glued to its unpainted identical backing, poke the feather between the layers:

Press birds flat with a book to let the glue dry and secure the feathers.

Taking turns, the children can outline the important parts of the design with glue and sprinkle on the glitter. (Don't let them get carried away with this, or the simplicity of the design will be lost!)

Display

Using circles of masking tape, arrange the large green feathers in a tree-like pattern on the wall:

Make a large pear out of yellow construction paper and place it in a nest of excelsior on one of the branches of the tree.

Animals in Unusual Settings

Scatter all the birds at random throughout the tree; if you have too many, put some down beside the trunk.

These "partridges" make attractive take-home Christmas tree decorations too. Find the balance point at the top of each bird and poke a paper clip hook through it as an ornament hanger.

Lesson 5
Donkeys and Dandelions

Donkeys and Dandelions

Donkeys, being rather comical animals, provide the kind of drawing subject that a child approaches eagerly and with confidence. Combining these donkeys with dandelions presents to the observer an alliteration and an incongruity which heightens the interest of the display.

Preparation

Borrow a "pin-the-tail-on-the-donkey" game and put it up at the front of the room. While the children are playing the game they will also be observing and remembering the form of the animal. This will aid and motivate the drawing process.

Presentation

After the excitement of the game has diminished, pass out 9" × 12" grey construction paper on which the drawings can be rendered in pencil. (The donkey game poster could be hung a bit higher and used as a model if requested.)

Suggest variations for the drawings such as: facing the donkey in another direction, running, sitting, different ear placement, etc.

While the children are cutting out their donkeys, pass out a small piece of black fabric (felt is best) to each. Two pointed, floppy ears are to be cut from the fabric and then attached to the donkey's head with glue. Black yarn cut in quarter-inch segments can be glued to the back of the neck for a mane, and could also be used for the tip of the tail. Eyes can be made of paper or simply applied with crayon.

To make the dandelions, each child will need a 6" × 9" piece of green paper and a 4 1/2" × 6" yellow piece. If dandelion flowers happen to be in bloom at the time it might be fun for the children to collect some specimens (both of flowers and leaves) and examine carefully their form, texture and color.

Cut the stem for the flower and top it with an oval of yellow. Glue tiers of thin yellow petals to the oval, beginning with the bottom tier and working toward the top for a textured effect:

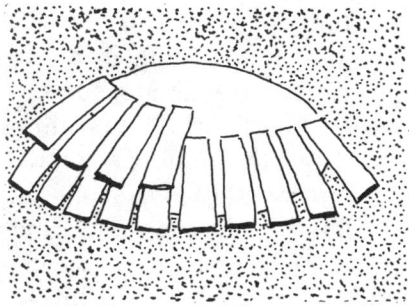

Make a giant drawing of the dandelion leaf on the chalk board:

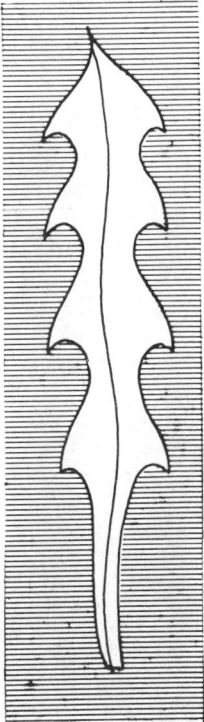

The students should draw several leaves on the green paper, matching the height to that of the flower. Then, using several different shades of green, crayon in the veins and textural accents. (It's easier to add the crayon before the leaves are cut out.)

Join flowers and leaves at the base of the flower stem with glue to complete the plant.

Display

Round off ten sheets of 12" × 18" black construction paper to look like hills. Place them in an overlapping pattern on a wall, starting with three hills at your eye level and working your way down toward the floor. The bottom row will be just about child's eye level. Tape the donkeys to the hills, scattering the smallest ones in the back and the large ones along the bottom of the display. The dandelions can be placed at random throughout, either in clusters or as single color-accents, whichever you deem more effective.

Identify the display by printing grade and room number on a small sign. Attach a string and let a large donkey carry it in its mouth.

Chapter 3. Houses for Looking Into

Lesson 1
Life in a Medieval Castle

Life in a Medieval Castle

Preparation

Without any explanation to your class, give each child a piece of 12" × 18" white drawing paper and tell him to cover it with black crayon lines:

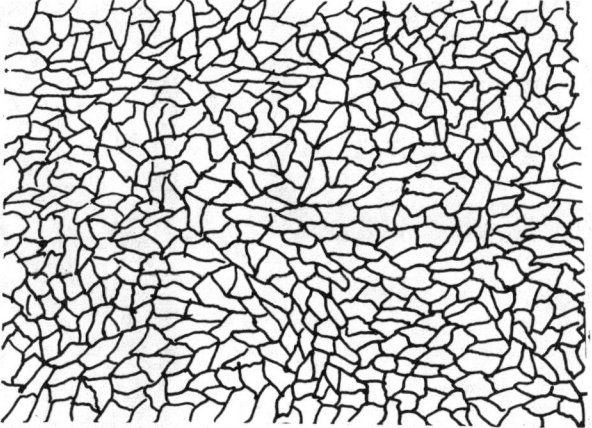

You should inform them that the lines are to look like the cracks between the stones in a wall, but keep the reason for the project as a surprise. The stone drawings will take only about ten minutes to complete, and the activity is a good quiet one for the end of a busy day.

After the children have gone home, start converting their work into a three-dimensional castle.

Cut Gothic windows (about 4 inches wide and 5 inches high) out of the middle of twelve of the sheets, then staple them into cylinders. Cut two more pieces in half lengthwise to make 4 crenelated walls:

Cut one piece into 4 lengthwise parts (also crenelated) to be used as bartizans.

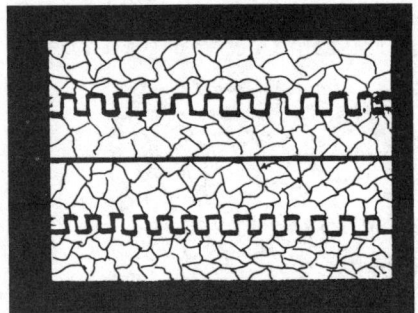

Houses for Looking Into

Put up the castle with circles of masking tape. Begin with the cylinders: tape one to the wall (at child's-eye level with its window facing a bit to the right. Attach a bartizan piece at the top and allow it to project out a bit all around the cylinder:

To the left of this completed turret, and exactly next to it, put up another cylinder with its window facing straight out. Top this one with a yellow paper cone. The next two turrets can be made twice as high as the first two simply by placing one cylinder on top of another. Top these with a narrow crenelated strip. Continue to create turrets of varying heights until you have exhausted your supply of cylinders. You can also vary the toppings with yellow paper cones.

Find the wall pieces and cut some more (but smaller) Gothic windows in them at different levels. Put the wall in front of the turrets, keeping the bases even. Attach it to the cylinders with tape; you can ripple it a bit to accentuate the three-dimensional effect.

Presentation

When the children come in the next day and see how you've transformed their stone-work into a castle, they will be eager to find out what comes next. You could use this project in conjunction with a full-scale study of medieval history, or you might prefer to keep it in the category of minimal time-line information. A lot depends on the age level of your group. In any case, *some* discussion of the medieval period will occur, and supplementary material should be made available. When the time is ripe for putting down on paper visually that which has been discussed verbally, pass out 9″ × 9″ white drawing paper. Students can draw their impressions of anything medieval people might be doing in any room of a castle. Drawings may be colored according to the child's preference of available materials. Tempera paint is usually most satisfactory, but crayons or colored pencils could be used instead. (Perhaps someone will want to include a knight among the array of costumes and will want to use silver foil as a medium.)

Display

Review all the completed drawings with the children. The group can decide which scenes are the most appropriate for the various parts of the castle. Slide the pictures into their designated spots inside the castle. Adjust the position so that the window allows maximum viewing of each scene, and then secure with tape.

For the final touch, make some brightly colored penant-shaped flags and attach them to soda straws. Print your grade and room number on the flags and poke them down through the tops of the yellow-cone towers.

Lesson 2
See-Into
Victorian Houses

See-Into Victorian Houses

Preparation

Prepare 3 giant houses by gluing or taping together 4 sheets of 12" × 18" construction paper for each one:

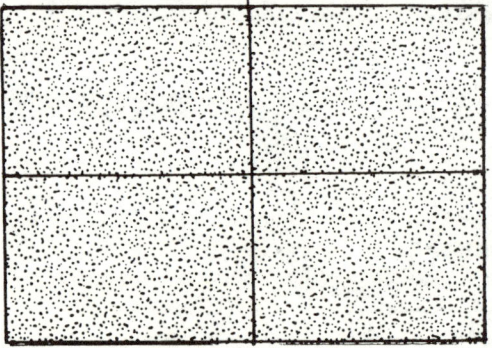

Add a variety of construction paper roofs:

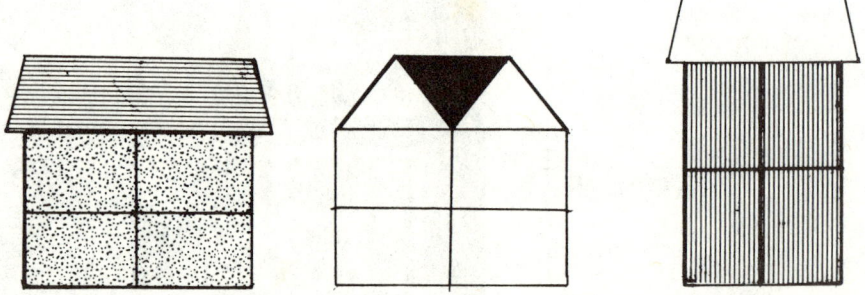

Cut out big windows and doors, and line the windows (from

Houses for Looking Into

the inside by *taping* on cellophane. (Glue won't work with cellophane.)

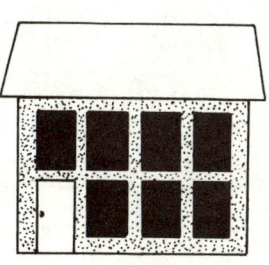  

Presentation

Show your house-structure to your class and discuss who might live in these homes and how tall the people would be. Give each child his choice of colored 9" × 12" construction paper and tell him to draw whatever and whomever he thinks could be seen through one of the windows. He should then add appropriate furniture and accessories and color his drawing (heavily) with crayon.

If more time and material were available, the rooms could be made out of cut-paper pieces from the scrap box, with real wallpaper glued to the walls.

Display

Decide which room-pictures are most appropriate for the available windows. (You may have to put up a quick addition such as a garage or recreation room.) Tape them to the backs of the houses in the window spaces.

Students who finish early may want to add final embellishments to the fronts of the houses with tempera paint and cut-paper, e.g., white frames around windows, decorations on doors, front stairs, chimney, flowerboxes.

Back the display with sky blue paper and add some cotton clouds. Finish off the fronts of the houses with a long line of paper grass.

Lesson 3
Giant Beehive

Giant Beehive

Creating these funny honey bees takes very little time and provides much of the inspiration for making their condominium-type, look-into hive.

Preparation

You will need black, yellow, orange and white 9" × 12" construction paper. Cut it into quarters 6" × 4" so that every child will have a piece of color. A pattern for the hexagonal hive sections will save time and insure their fitting together when displayed. Three to five prepared patterns should be enough for the average group.

Presentation

Draw an oval on the yellow for the bee's body. Cut it out and add some curved stripes with a black crayon.

Houses for Looking Into

Cut a circular shape from the black for the head (it should be about half the size of the body), and glue it in place. Add two white circles for eyes and give them black centers.

Legs, feet, nose, hat, etc. may be cut from the orange paper, and the children will think of interesting things to add, using any remaining scraps of the other colors. Heavy-duty plastic makes unusual wings, but lacking that, they can be cut from the white paper and then lightly veined with brown crayon.

Pass out the patterns and tell each child to draw and cut out two hexagons from colored paper. One will be used to make the interior of his bee's room and the other will be the lift-up covering. The room's furnishings could be either drawn in crayon or made from scrap box paper. If drawn in crayon, then a wash (tempera diluted with an equal amount of water) can be brushed over the drawing to heighten the color by contrast.

When each room is completed, attach the second hexagon at the top with paper hinges. This allows it to be opened and closed like a writing tablet. When hung on the wall, the room interiors will be hidden until the covering is lifted.

Display

Begin hanging the hive sections on the wall at a point that is about a foot below a child's eye level. Continue to fit the sections together both above and below the first one; none should be too high to be opened by a child, however. Your "hive" will probably end up being a great deal wider than it is high; this will leave plenty of space above it for the bees. Place them in a random flight formation which could extend all the way up to the ceiling. If each child has made two bees, you might have enough of them to extend across the ceiling and on to the opposite wall.

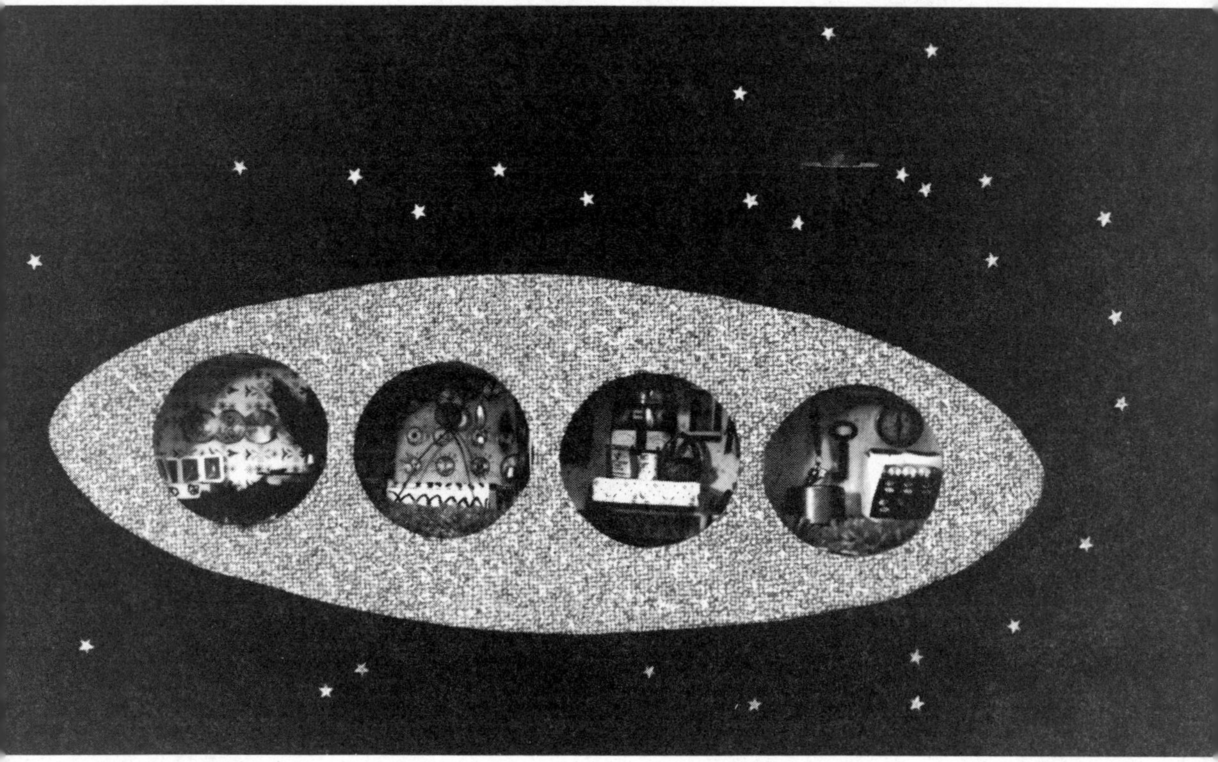

Lesson 4
Life Aboard a U.F.O.

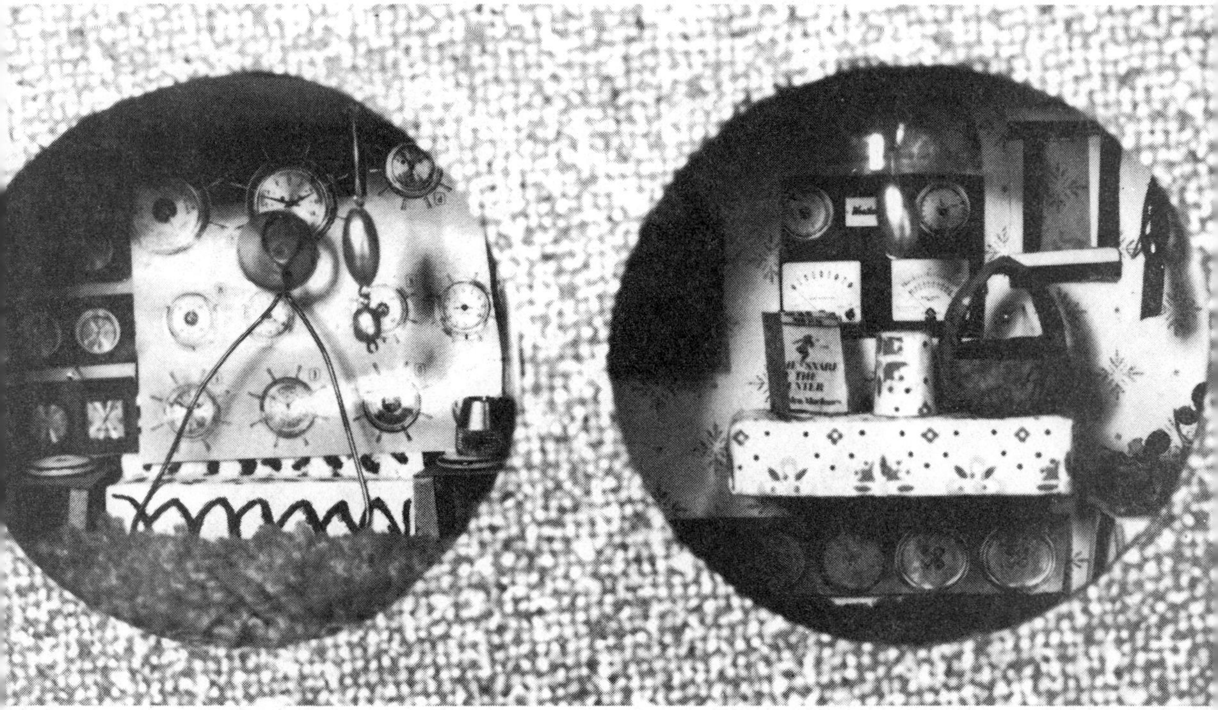

Life Aboard a U.F.O.

Creatures from planets other than our own may or may not have visited earth. The controversy may rage outside your room while you and your class put together some very funny examples of "U.F.O.s."

Preparation

Make 3 large space ships from heavy cardboard. Begin by cutting a pattern for yourself from a full-sized sheet of newspaper or a piece of shelf paper. Fold the paper and mark off a 30″ line along the fold. Mark 4 dots along the fold at 6″ intervals. Set a compass for a 2-1/2 inch radius and draw 4 semicircles along the paper with the compass point centered at each dot:

Keep the paper folded and cut out the space ship.

Houses for Looking Into

Now find three good stiff sheets of cardboard large enough to accommodate your pattern. (Sides of packing boxes are a good source.) Draw your pattern three times and cut it out, using heavy duty scissors or a razor knife. Glue wallpaper or construction paper to one side of each ship and trim. The round windows could be filled with clear cellophane if you like.

Presentation

Define "U.F.O." and discuss with your class some funny possibilities of life on imaginary planets and what kind of spacecraft interiors these "people" might construct for a trip to earth. Would they use materials in the same way we do? Would their rooms be different or similar to ours? Bizarre ideas will make the most interesting projects.

Let the children pair themselves off so that each two friends will construct a room together. They should begin with a five-sided box. (An empty 48 tea-bag box with the lid cut off is the perfect size.) Put out all of the scrap materials you own, such as: wallpaper remnants, carpet scraps, empty thread spools, junk jewelry, twigs of wood, fabric scraps, beads, nuts, toothpicks, cellophane, buttons, feathers and, of course, colored construction paper.

The wall-covering should go on first; it should be applied to the box's bottom and two sides so that the remaining sides will become floor and ceiling. Floor covering should be fitted next, and finally, furniture and accessories fastened in place:

Houses for Looking Into

Some students may wish to put "people" into the setting. These creatures could be assembled from pipe cleaners, styrofoam packing pieces, fabric, yarn, etc.

Display

Tape each room securely in place behind the round windows of the cardboard space ships. The eight children involved with each ship can pool their ideas as to any final touches to be added. Perhaps a TV antenna, clothesline, headlights, stairs, chimney, mailbox or other amusing incongruities would appeal to the group.

Pin the U.F.O.s to a bulletin board which has been covered with black paper. Each will require at least eight straight pins pushed right through the backs of the rooms at an angle. Stars can be glued to the black paper as a finishing touch to the display.

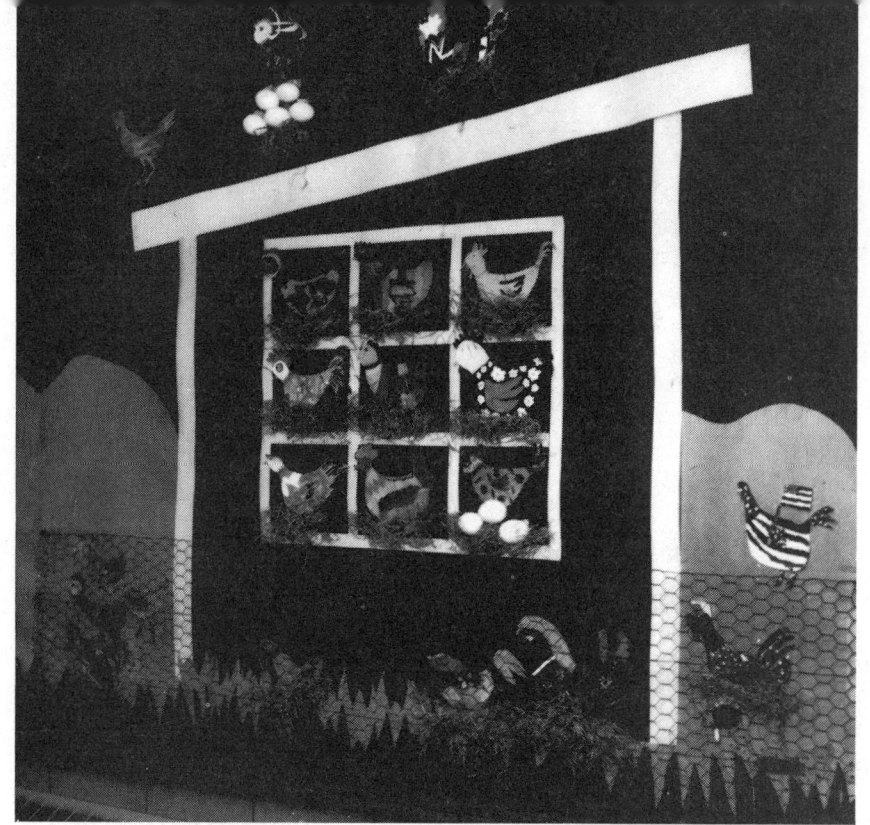

Lesson 5
Henhouse

Henhouse

This project looks complicated but is really very simple once all materials have been assembled.

Preparation

Put up a large henhouse on a bulletin board or wall. Begin by tacking up six pieces of 9″ × 12″ black construction paper:

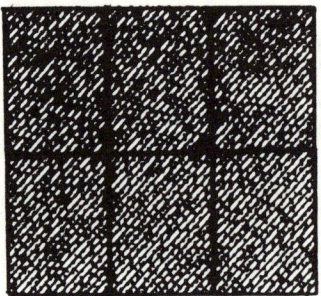

Cut some 1″ strips of white and fasten them around and between the black paper to define nine window spaces:

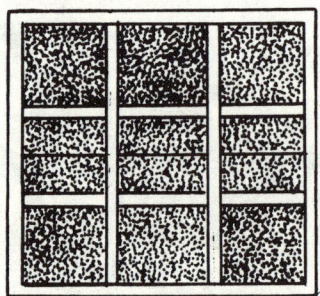

Border the entire window with 9″ × 12″ sheets of red paper. Then place a series of white strips across the top in a diagonal line to represent a slanting henhouse roof. (Cut off the excess red paper showing on top of the roof.)

Place a border of white strips around the red, and then top the slanting roof line with black to represent shingles.

Presentation

Tell the class that this is a henhouse and they are to make some very unusual chickens which will live here. Put some basic chicken shapes on the chalkboard:

Houses for Looking Into

Pass out 6" × 9" white drawing paper and encourage each child to make not only the shape but some design-like line divisions within the shapes. (The pencil lines can be gone over with black markers if available.)

Decide what colors of tempera will be needed and then get them ready. The more wildly the chickens are colored, the more interesting they will become. Of course care should be taken that they are done neatly. Cut them out when the paint is dry.

Display

Put a small excelsior nest in each window. This can be attached to the paper with masking tape (the color of which blends right into that of the excelsior). If you are using a bulletin board for this display, the excelsior can be attached with straight pins. Put some of the nests along the ground in front of the henhouse. For a large class, you might even need to use the roof to accommodate all of the chickens. Set a chicken in each nest along with some blown-out egg shells which you or the children have saved. If you can find about 7 feet of chicken wire, use it across the lower half of the display.

The eggshells could be wildly colored with the tempera too if this project is being done around Easter time. After all, as the children will point out, colored hens lay colored eggs!

Chapter 4. Pictures in Varied Shapes

Lesson 1
Paintings on Real Leaves

Paintings on Real Leaves

Here is a painless way to get yourself in gear for the starting of school. It preserves some of the last precious days of summer vacation and arms you with a good fall art project to which you can look forward.

Gather about 40 green leaves. (Any variety will do if their size is about half the area of your hand). Do this before the leaves have begun to change color, and then press them in a book and forget about them for a month.

Preparation

Open 27 jars of tempera. (Three each of black, white, yellow, brown, green, blue, purple, red and orange). Gather together the same number of the smallest paint brushes in your school, one brush for each jar. Cut 6 plastic drinking straws in one-inch segments and tape one segment to the side of each jar to function as a brush holder so that the same brush stays with the same jar throughout the project. Place all the paint on an empty desk, and then get our your well-pressed summer leaves.

Presentation

Pass one leaf to each child and emphasize the fragile quality. By now you know your group well enough so that you can decide how much fantasy they might want to employ in their role of "Leaf Painters." Present an array of choices from simply coloring the leaf, to painting a simple subject on it, to painting a very carefully executed miniature picture on it. (Those who take the simplest options might want to do 2 or 3 leaves in order to achieve self-satisfaction; hence the necessity for the extra leaves). If a *picture* is to be painted, then a small practice sketch on paper may be helpful to those students who need more confidence.

The fragile quality of the leaves precludes any kind of preliminary pencil outline; the paint is applied directly to the surface one color at a time. (Don't worry if the wet paint tends to make the leaves curl up a bit. They will flatten down nicely later.)

After the leaves have been painted and dried, trim some 9" × 12" sheets of colored construction paper to 8" × 11". Cross-cut these into 4" × 5-1/2" quarters and pass them out to the students. Each child should position and glue his leaf to the paper. Collect all and press in a book overnight so that they dry flat.

Display

Cut sheets of 9" × 12" black paper into quarters and attach each mounted leaf so that the black will frame the colored paper evenly, with the leaf in the center. Add three strips of black to the back to simulate an easel tripod. (This job can be done by the children themselves, a student art committee, or by student aides.)

Cut a painter's palette from light brown construction paper and paint color blobs around the inside edge with tempera. In the center, paint your room number and a display title such as: "The Jack Frost Painters Present This Year's New Fall Leaves." Add an elf's face above it if you like. Tape the palette to the wall and arrange the leaf-easels around it. Several smaller easel-forms cut from colored construction paper could be interspersed among the leaf-paintings to pull the display together.

Lesson 2
Raindrops

Raindrops

Preparation

The raindrop shape to be used for this lesson should be about six inches long and four inches wide. It can be drawn free-hand by each student (or presented as a pattern) on white drawing paper.

Presentation

Cut out the shapes and ask the class to imagine these to be huge magnifying raindrops which belong to the same shower. What scenes might be captured or reflected inside them? Where are they falling? What time of the year is it?

The students should render their drawings in pencil, taking care to erase as few times as possible, to prepare them for coloring. This lesson lends itself well to the use of water colors and, if that medium is available, by all means encourage your students to try it. When the paint is thoroughly dry, the parts of the picture may be outlined with black ink lines for emphasis. (Lacking water color materials, crayons or colored pencils could be used instead.) Back each raindrop with black paper and cut out again, leaving a quarter inch of black edge as a border.

Display

Put up a life-sized face at a place on the wall that is way below eye level. You can make the face of cut paper or paint it with water colors. Add yarn hair, a hat and a scarf or tie. Tape up the raindrops at random, starting a little above the face and working toward the ceiling. Grey clouds go across the top of the display as the source of the raindrops. Large hunks of pulled-apart steel wool make dandy clouds, and if you're on friendly terms with your custodian you might borrow some. It will still be usable after the display has been taken down.

Variation

Instead of a water color picture, let each raindrop shape be the vehicle for a cut-paper colored flower. Tape blue cellophane over the flower and give each raindrop a blue paper border rather than a black one.

Put a row of paper grass and flowers along the bottom of the display and some white styrofoam clouds (packing pieces glued to white paper cloud-shapes) across the top. Between the grass and clouds, string up five or six lengths of blue yarn on a slant and attach your raindrops (also on a slant) to the yarn.

The display title may be placed across the clouds in the form of large cut-paper letters which spell out "APRIL SHOWERS BRING..."

Lesson 3
Star Worlds

Star Worlds

Preparation

The purpose of this lesson is to project the challenge of making a picture conform to a star shape. For that reason little preparation is needed except to cut some 9″ × 9″ pieces of white drawing paper for the class. You may also want to make a star pattern out of tag board. This would be handy to help those students who might become absolutely frustrated if they cannot draw a star. Rather than allow any student to be completely turned off at the beginning of this project, use a pattern.

Presentation

After the star shape has been outlined on the paper, ask the children to imagine that this is another world that they are looking into. Things are happening here which may make no sense at all to most people in our world, but which are an everyday part of this star world. Creatures who live there might in some way be influenced by the fact that their world consists of straight lines and no curves. Their lives may have purpose and meaning to them, but at first glance seem meaningless to "real" people. Their homes would be shaped much differently from ours and even the way in which they use their homes might be unlike our definitions of home functions.

The pictures should be started in pencil. Composition will require very little pruning since the star shape does it naturally, and the drawing stage should progress rather rapidly because of this. Go over the finished pencil drawing with india ink or (black) ball-point pen; then set out tempera paints, and since a rapid exchange of many colors will be necessary, use the method described in the first lesson of this chapter.

After the paintings are dry, cut around the star shape, glue to black paper, and cut out again leaving a black surrounding edge.

Display

Star worlds need a star-gazing wizard looking at them through a magnifying telescope. You can make your wizard's face from pink paper (in profile) and then add hair, beard and sideburns with dark carpet scraps (if you have any), wooly fabric or construction paper. His cape can be fashioned from construction paper more easily than from fabric, but a fabric cloak would definitely be more interesting. Make a large pointy hat by stapling a 12" ×18" piece of construction paper into a cone shape. Flatten the back of the cone where it will be taped to the wall, and decorate the front of it with stars of bright colors. The wizard's telescope is made by cutting four 3" × 9" strips of paper from a 9" × 12" sheet. Staple each strip into a cylinder shape with gradually diminishing diameters. Telescope the cylinders one inside the other and secure with tape.

Tape the wizard to the wall close to the floor and position his hand-held telescope so that it points in a line from his eye toward the stars. These are put up in a random pattern at child's eye level for close scrutiny.

Lesson 4
Lift-Up-Object Paintings

Lift-Up-Object Paintings

Preparation

Hardly any preparation is necessary for this project. Once you've amassed an assortment of construction paper colors (9″ × 12″ size), tempera paints, 9″ × 12″ white drawing paper, and your class, there's nothing to do except begin.

Presentation

Students should think of an object that represents some strong interest of theirs. Just about anything will be suitable as long as it is not greatly latticed or perforated and is formed in good proportion to the paper, i.e., not extremely thin and elongated. All this will become clear later. Suggestions from you will probably not be needed by the greater portion of the class, but you'd better be prepared for the child who scrunches up his nose, bangs his pencil flat on his desk, and announces "I can't think of anything." *He* really does need help, especially when his peers are busily at work around him, each drawing an object in pencil on the white paper. Some whispered suggestions might be: a roller skate, wheelbarrow, beach ball, scuba mask, pencil sharpener, book, etc. Avoid suggesting baseballs, footballs or racing cars because at least two boys in the class will already be drawing these, and they may think you a traitor in an apparent betrayal of their ideas.

The drawings should utilize a good portion of the paper so that they are large enough to carry sufficient fine details to make them interesting. Care should be taken in the painting phase so that the finished product is neat and very pleasant to look at. When paint is dry the objects should be cut out.

This project is one that will require several separate sessions, both to keep motivation freshly renewed and to avoid crowding the time schedule into an undesirable "hurry-up" atmosphere. Work should progress almost leisurely.

The second phase involves the use of the colored paper. Let each child choose his own paper; having done so, he should center his finished object-painting on it and trace carefully around it. This is the outline in which he will make a picture. The picture will show the environment to which the object relates. Once again, for the child who needs help in the form of suggestions: the picture inside the roller skate shape would be one of children skating. The wheelbarrow shape would lend itself nicely to a picture of a garden. The beach ball shape could contain some people surfing. The scuba mask shape would, of course, show an underwater composition. The pencil sharpener or book could be a classroom scene. Encourage the children to include people and animals in their drawings for greater interest. Paint the pictures with tempera and let dry.

The last phase of the project is to position the object precisely on top of the picture and hinge them together at the top with a small rectangle of paper.

OPEN

CLOSED

Pictures in Varied Shapes

The hinge is secured with glue on the underside of the top of the object, then poked through a slit at the top of the picture and finally secured with glue on the back of the picture paper.

As a final touch, the edges of the paper may be scalloped or cut in some other decorative way and then edged with tempera.

Display

Put the completed picture-units on the wall in a random pattern. They should be low enough so that children can easily reach out, lift up the object on its hinge, and view the picture beneath.

Lesson 5
Paintings in a Basket

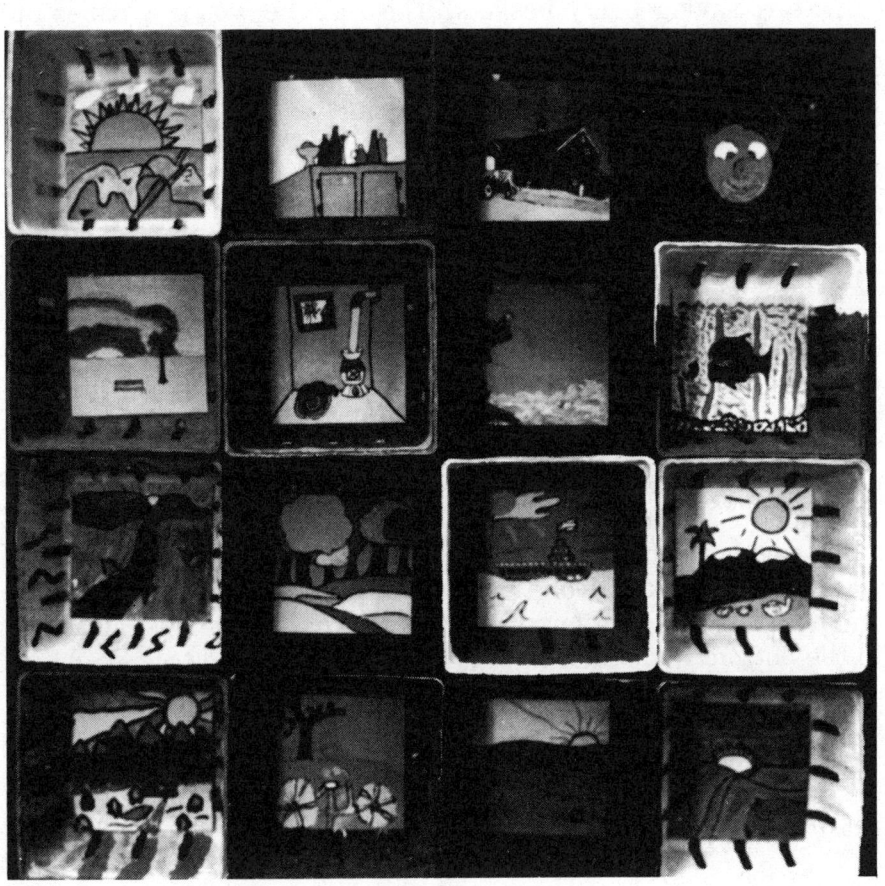

Paintings in a Basket

Preparation

Start saving berry baskets. They can be wooden, paper or plastic, but decide which type you're going to work with and then ask your class to bring some in too. When you have enough for all, you're ready to start the project.

Presentation

The baskets are to be used as frames for very tiny pictures. The pictures should be painted first; for each child, you will need a piece of white drawing paper which has been cut to fit the bottom of the basket. The pictures should be kept simple and can be rendered in water colors, tempera, or colored pencils. (Crayons are not very usable in this project, since they are too blunt.)

The baskets should be used to frame and to enhance the colors of the picture. The cardboard baskets can simply be painted, either with solid colors or designs. Care *should* be taken, however, to avoid having the basket become more important than the picture.

Wooden baskets look fine just as they are. The natural color and texture make an effective setting for any picture; just attach it to the bottom with glue.

The plastic baskets can be changed by weaving narrow stripes of colored construction paper in and out of the openings in a basket-weave operation. The colors used for the weaving should be limited to two. (This is a useful technique for making Easter baskets too; just attach a handle.)

Display

Glue or tape the pictures to the bottom of each basket. They can then be arranged on the wall in either a square or a random pattern. They could also be joined back to back and suspended from the ceiling either in pairs or groups of pairs.

Chapter 5. Textured Semi-3-D Animals

Lesson 1
Shaggy Carpet-Scrap Lions

Shaggy Carpet-Scrap Lions

Preparation

Cut a 3-inch "rounded square" of shag carpet scrap (all the same color) for each child.

Choose a color of construction paper close to the color of the carpeting and count out a 9″ × 12″ sheet for the lion's body for each child.

Cut a 4½″ × 6″ piece of that same color for each lion's head. (You get 4 pieces from a 9″ × 12″ sheet of paper).

Cut a 3″ length of thin rope for each tail.

Presentation

Talk about the shaggy texture of the lion's mane and tail and compare this to the carpet scraps and rope sections. Then expand the concept of texture to that of sound, and allot a little fun time to "growling practice."

Show on the chalk board how the face can be drawn in pencil on the small rectangle of construction paper:

Begin with a triangle for the nose and bring out 2 curved lines for the muzzle.

Go up from the corners of the nose for the eyebrows.

Textured Semi-3-D Animals

Then set in the eye outlines at a slant. Connect muzzle to eyebrow and then round off the top of the head:

Fill in iris and pupils, and with a *white* crayon color in the whites of the eyes.

Choose a color of crayon for the iris and color them in.

Now, using a black crayon, go over all the pencil lines heavily and accurately. Fill in the nose triangle and the pupils of the eyes.

Make eyelashes and a *few* dots on the muzzle for whisker follicles.

Cut out the face and glue to the center of the carpet scrap.

Fold the 9" × 12" piece of construction paper in half "the short way" and keep the fold at the top.

Draw the lion's body and cut out while keeping the paper folded.

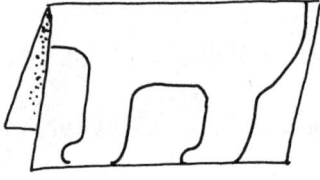

Crayon in some partition lines for toes. Attach head and tail (fray out the end of the tail).

Display

Back the bulletin board with "sky" and hills (rounded off construction paper segments).

Add a large round colored cellophane sun and some colored overlapping cloud-forms to the sky.

Make some palm trees of telescoped carton sections (trunk) and feathers (palm leaves).

Pin the lions to the hills and allow all 4 legs of each to show to complete the semi-3-D effect.

Lesson 2
Fabric and Paper Turtles

Fabric and Paper Turtles

Preparation

Fabric scraps need to be cut to the shape of turtle shells. These can be prepared by the students, student aides, or by yourself. It all depends upon the ages of your children. Very young children (kindergarten and first grades) cannot cut fabric with scissors of any kind. Second and third graders can manage the operation but must be provided with super-sharp long-blade scissors (such as desk scissors: yours plus some extra pairs borrowed from the teachers next door.) Fourth graders can cut through *anything* with *anything* and therefore no preparation will be needed for them. But a plan for the fabric-shell-cutting must precede the lesson presentation, and of course the fabric itself must be available.

Presentation

Discuss the fact that turtles' heads, legs and tails, are all projections from the shell. (The students will all know this, so let *them* tell you.) Much anecdotal information will certainly follow, and as it proceeds, you can be passing around the fabric (or the pre-cut shells) plus a 6" × 9" piece of black construction paper.

The finished shells should be glued to the middle of the horizontally positioned paper. Using a yellow or white crayon, demonstrate how to draw in head, tail and feet.

Pass out tiny pieces of white paper from which an oval for the eye is to be cut. When this has been glued in place, cut a small black circle for the inside of the eye.

Invite the children to add any individual details that they find

either decorative or amusing to their turtles. Media for this final-touch operation may include scrap paper and crayon; the time allotment should be short.

Display

You will want to create a facsimile of a boggy swamp for these turtles. (You might even consider utilizing some space adjacent to a drinking fountain . . . the remote relationship amuses all ages!) Look in your dried weed collection and see how close you can come to cattails. (If you have the real thing, that will be terrific!) Tape the weeds to the wall in a nicely fanned-out clump, and then cover the tape with a free-form shape which you've cut from orange paper:

Continue to add similar free form shapes. Work around and away from the first one; use any colors you like. Overlap the forms occasionally for variety. Intersperse the turtles, and tape them securely; they will be rather weighty because of their fabric shells.

Top off the display with a few dragonflies (which could have been made by students who finished before the rest of the class):

and then add some nice, white, fringy clouds which announce your grade and room number.

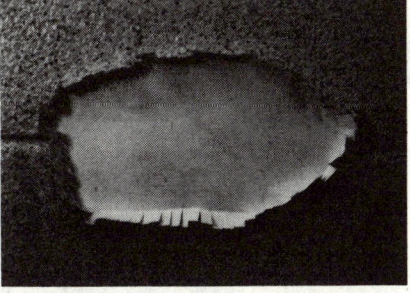

Go ahead; be brave—put it up by a drinking fountain!

Textured Semi-3-D Animals

Lesson 3
Plastic-Packing-Pieces Rabbits

Plastic-Packing-Pieces Rabbits

Preparation

Just about any shape of plastic packing material will work for this project as long as it is white. You will need at least a 12″ cubic boxful—maybe more for a very large class. Before beginning the rabbits, make the wall:

Spread out a discarded white window shade on the floor. Pour a small quantity of red tempera paint into a shallow dish and dip the entire side of a (softened with water) rectangular sponge in the paint. Press the painty side of the sponge evenly and gently along the top of the window shade. This will leave a textured rectangular print which resembles a brick. Repeat the process to the end of the row and allow narrow, white, vertical, bonding spaces to show between each brick. Alternate the rows to produce a transverse pattern, and continue the operation until the unit is complete.

The wall could be made by students working individually during "free-time" or by student aides if your class consists of very young children.

Presentation

Put up the wall, accompanied by any daffodils which might have been left over from the alligator project (chapter 2, lesson 1).

Pass a 12″ × 18″ piece of white construction to each student and explain that they are going to produce some rabbits which will be looking over the top of the wall, so that only the heads and ears will show. The forms will first be cut from the white paper and then the plastic packing pieces will be glued on for texture.

Since there will be a great deal of time consumed by the mechanics of this project, it is best to divide the group into two parts and then later combine their products:

Group I makes the head and paws:

Group II will make the cheeks and ears:

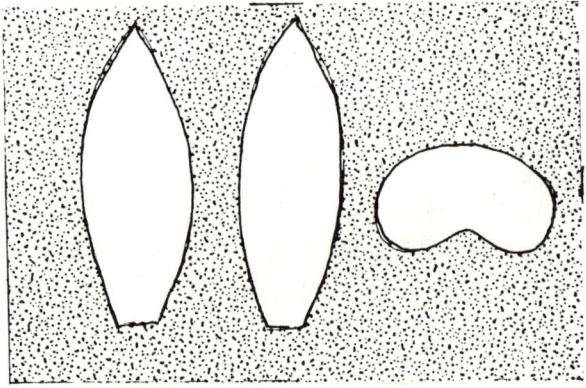

The plastic will have to be broken up in small pieces to fill out tiny corners. Work progresses more smoothly if the glue is applied first to the paper (a 4" square area at a time) and then the plastic material pressed into it. Nothing will seem to be stuck until the glue is thoroughly dry, and for that reason, the pieces should be left flat and undisturbed for at least an hour after positioning.

While the glue is setting, the additional parts for the faces can be prepared.

Group I makes the eyes out of black and white paper. Group II makes ear inserts and noses from pink paper.

Assemble the rabbit parts according to their varying sizes as well as the friendships of the children from each of the two groups. Add some broomstraw whiskers and some pastel colored neck bows, then tape each rabbit together securely at the back of each unit.

Display

Pin up some large, light-blue cloud shapes above the wall. Insert some large brush-branches in front of the clouds (but in back of the wall). Prune the branches so that their backs are flat and flush with the bulletin board. Secure them with tape (or wire and nails, if you have to).

Put up a row of rabbit faces along the wall, placing their paws so that they appear to be hanging out over it. Fit in a second row of faces in back of the first; if you run out of space, a third tier may be necessary.

For final touches, add some bits of grass, or a birdhouse or kite in one of the branches.

Lesson 4
Toothpick Porcupines

Toothpick Porcupines

Preparation

Find some light brown paper in the 9" × 12" size and cut it into quarters. Repeat this operation with black paper so that each child may be furnished with two 4½" × 6" pieces of paper: one of black and one of brown.

Buy several boxes of rounded wooden toothpicks. (Each child will use at least 20, and they are packed 250 to a box.) The last bit of preparation will be to sort out some styrofoam packing pieces of such a shape and quantity so that they will hold in place the 20 toothpicks when they are jabbed into the porcupines.

Presentation

Pass out all the materials except the toothpicks. Begin to draw the porcupine on the brown paper. Explain that it is something like the shape of a lemon, and that the pointy nub on a lemon would correspond to the porcupine's nose. Cut out the shape and glue it temporarily to the black paper. Only one drop of glue should be used here just enough to keep it from slippping but not so much as to fasten it permanently. Cut around the edge of the brown shape, leaving a quarter inch of black edging showing all around. Pull the brown shape apart from the black and glue the pieces of styrofoam to the back. This entire unit then is reglued to the black paper, thus creating a kind of "styrofoam sandwich."

While the body is drying, make the eyes. A very tiny quantity of white paper will be needed for this, in addition to the (leftover) scraps of black. Cut a circle of white, and glue to that a smaller insert of black. Sunglasses are a neat and amusing addition to the porcupines, since they will be basking in the sun. Tiny scraps of cellophane would be useful here, or simply use clear tape.

Pass out the toothpicks (20 to each student) and demonstrate the most effective position and angle for their placement.

Some students may wish to use more toothpicks, but this should be approached with caution since the styrofoam will hold only so many without cracking.

Display

Use a sun left over from some other display, or make a new one. Make a sun-umbrella too (large enough to shelter two or three porcupines), and put it up at an angle to the sun. Let several paper-strip rays emanate from the sun toward free-form orange color splashes on the ground. Scatter some weed clusters here and there among the color splashes, and your display background is ready to feature the porcupines.

Lesson 5
Rope Camels

Rope Camels

Preparation

Practice drawing a camel so that you will be able to give your students a good beginning for their drawings. Block it out first in simple geometric shapes:

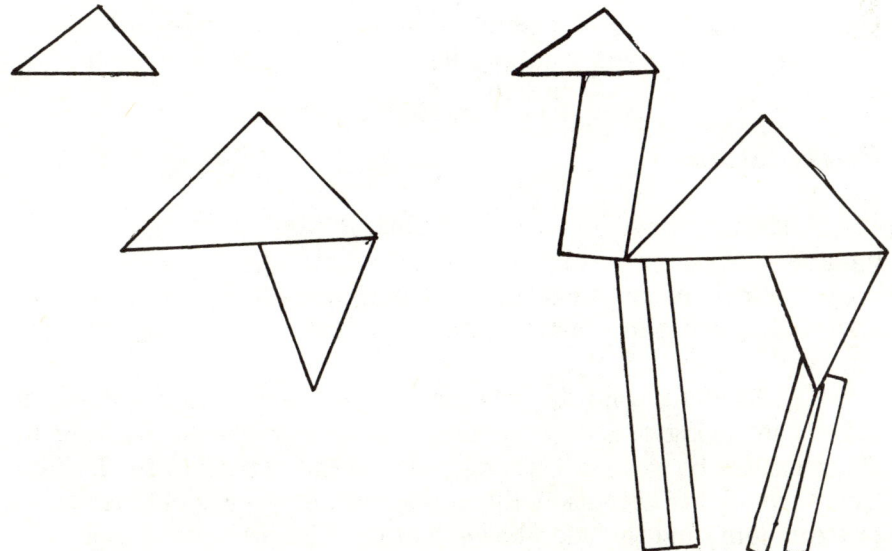

Three triangles . . . and four rectangles.

Use the blocked-in version of your drawing as a guideline for the addition of curves and details:

Textured Semi-3-D Animals

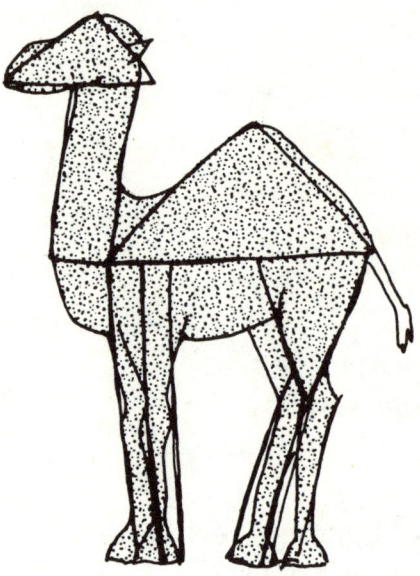

Find some rope (or heavy twine)—the brownish kind with a rough and scratchy fiber content. Cut the rope in three-inch segments so that there will be one piece for each child. In addition to the rope, you need only supply light brown construction paper of the 9" × 12" size.

Presentation

After the paper has been distributed, you might ask the class members to share their knowledge of camels. This discussion might be done in conjunction with a geography unit, and the differences between the Bactrian and Arabian camels may be emphasized.

The students may best begin to draw with pencil while you help them along the way by executing a very large drawing in chalk on the board. As this progresses, call attention to the fact that a camel has exceptionally long eyelashes because of his sandy environment, and the wide-based foot is such for the same reason.

The students can, at this point, go over the pencil lines with brown crayon and fill in the hump and neck with brown. Eyes, nostrils and ears can be emphasized with a heavy application of black crayon.

Distribute the rope segments while the drawings are being cut

out. The rope should be frayed out, pulled apart, and then applied with glue to those sections of the camel where he is shaggy: top of the head, chin, back and feet. (Some children will devise different patterns for the rope application; the more they depart from representational, the more decorative the effect will be.)

Display

Cover the top half of your bulletin board with an orange paper sky and the lower half with a yellow (or beige if you have it) desert.

Add a very large sun, made either from dark orange or cellophane, and some yellow clouds.

Cut a dozen dunes from sheets of sandpaper (or yellow construction paper), and arrange them along the horizon line. A few sand dunes could be placed a little lower and in front of the horizon to break up the foreground space more effectively.

Make several palm trees for an oasis effect. Cut three to five leaves for each from fabric scraps or carpet scraps and attach them at the top of a cork or bark trunk (salvaged pieces from a cork bulletin board or large sections of actual tree bark if you happen to have any).

Pin up the camels among the dunes, palm trees and flat sand foreground. An interesting final touch could be added in the form of an Arab tent or two. These could be made by students in conjunction with a social studies unit. Tent shapes can be simply cut from striped fabric, using a picture from the geography book as a guide.

Lesson 6
Cone Creatures

Cone Creatures

Preparation

Practice making a small paper cone; to do it the easiest way, use a compass. Set the radius at six inches and draw a half circle on a piece of 9" × 12" construction paper. Cut it out and then shape it into a cone. The perforation left by your compass point will become the point of the cone; you can overlap the straight edges as far as you like to decrease the cone's diameter. (You might want to make several more of these semicircles for your students to use as patterns if you do not have a good supply of compasses for them.)

Further lesson preparation would involve getting out your entire collection of scrap material such as carpet, fabric, junk jewelry, buttons, feathers, glitter, and various paper tissue, foil and colored construction paper.

Presentation

Demonstrate the cone-making procedure and then provide the class members with paper to make their own cones. Pass out paper clips to function as clamps to hold the paper together while the glue is drying. Explain that eventually they will be transforming the cones into creatures which will be entirely imaginary. These creatures might have faces, hands, and feet or multiples of these. They may be wearing clothes, or they may have a furry or fuzzy body covering. They may be wearing a uniform denoting a trade or profession, or they could even be wearing some sort of costume. Display the array of scrap materials and encourage the children to select odd bits and use them imaginatively.

As the cone creatures are being formed, cut some 4" × 18" lengths of paper, one for each child. These will be the loops in which the cones live. The loops are made by gluing the strip into a circular form and then folding it in two places.

The loops can be decorated to serve the needs or personality of the cone who lives there. Windows can be cut in the sides; carpeting could be glued to the floor. Pictures could be painted to grace the walls. As the loops are being constructed and decorated, care should be taken not to overcrowd the space to the point where the cone will not fit inside. If necessary, the loops can be widened by adding an extra length of paper.

Display

These projects can be very effectively displayed on bookcase shelves, tables, or window sills. Just cover the surface with brightly colored paper and let the children arrange their creations in groups. If you lack that kind of space, however, they can be hung on a wall. The display will be more striking but also more time consuming.

Begin the wall display by drawing several vertical rows of chalk dots. Put four or five dots in each row. They should be about 10 inches apart, and the rows should have about 10 inches between them. One dot is for each project. On each dot tape a paper clip pulled out to an L shape.

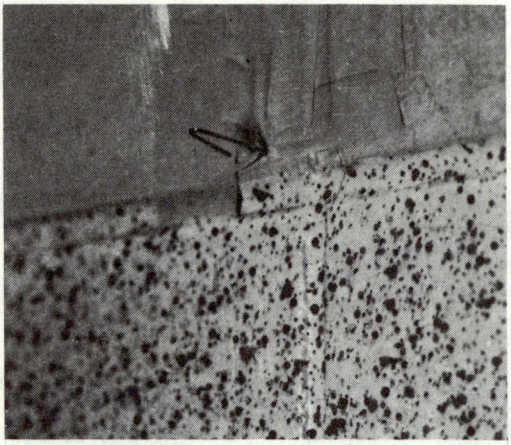

Cover the rows vertically with strips of paper. Tape the paper to the wall and let the projecting part of each paper clip poke through.

Hang the loops on the paper clips and secure with tape on the inside to prevent slipping. Some of the cones with a high center of gravity may require additional fastening to keep them from falling to the floor.

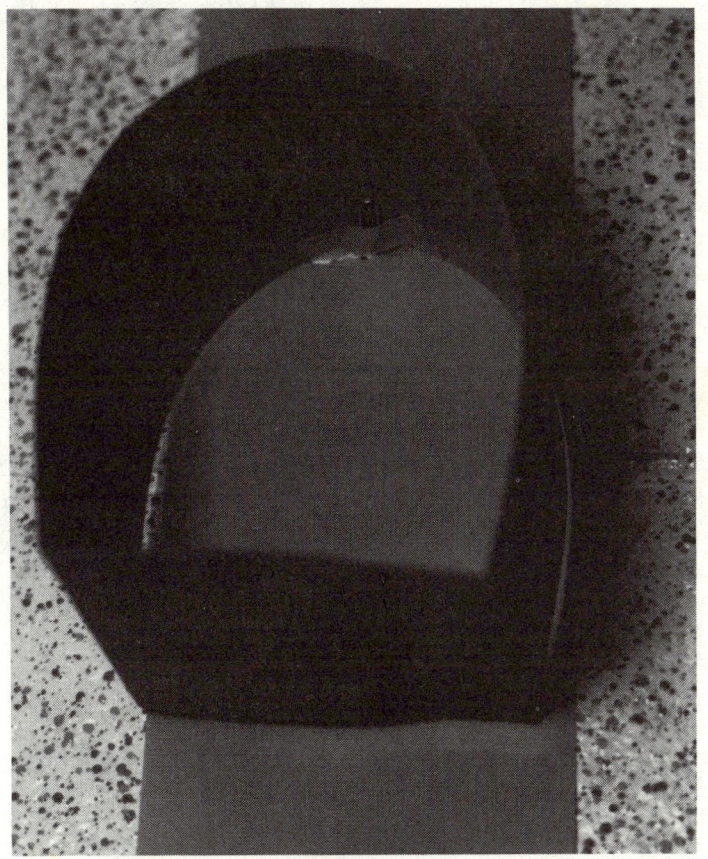

Textured Semi-3-D Animals

Lesson 7
Caterpillars & Co.

Caterpillars & Co.

Preparation

Cut several circles from cardboard to be used as patterns. Two inches in diameter is a good size; you'll need one pattern for every five children. You will also need some pennies to use as patterns, one of these for each child.

Cut some 9" × 12" yellow construction paper in half so that each member of your class will have a 6" × 9" sheet. Then prepare quarter pieces of 9" × 12" paper in the following colors: orange, white and black, and cut some orange yarn into lengths of about a foot.

Look through your carpet-scrap collections and see if you have any of the flexible rubber-backed kind. Pull out a long strip of it and round off one end with your desk scissors to create the head of a snake. Then cut the other end to a point for its tail. Add large paper eyes complete with light blue eye lids and lashes and then dot the front of the face with a gum-eraser nose. (If you do not have the carpet scrap available, you could use construction paper, a plait of rope, a folded piece of heavy fabric, or a segment of garden hose.)

Presentation

Drape the snake around anything anywhere in your room, and then present it as a stimulus for the making of other kinds of "things that creep." Caterpillars might be mentioned as a possible subject (and it might be best to swing into action right away in

their construction so that you don't end up with thirty or so disappointed, potential snake-creators). Pass out the cardboard patterns, the pennies and all the paper. Those children who've received the patterns should begin to draw six yellow circles and one white circle, and then pass the pattern on to someone else who does the same upon receiving it. Everyone else should draw around the penny five times on the orange paper and cut out the circles (which gives them something to do while they are waiting their turns with the cardboard patterns).

When every child has completed this much, he should have finished six large yellow circles, one large white circle, and five small orange ones. Now things start to get more interesting and more complicated. Glue a small orange circle to five of the yellow ones in an off-center position. This leaves one of the yellow circles plain. Cut the white circle in half and then in quarters. One white quarter is placed on the remaining yellow circle to create the white of the eye:

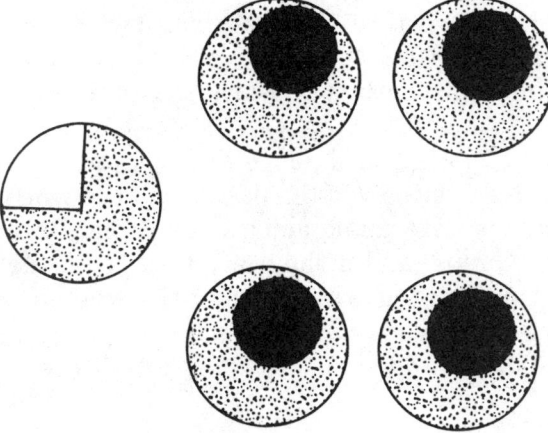

Cut a long quarter-inch strip from the remaining white paper and divide it into ten leg segments. Cut an eyeball, a nose, and ten shoes from the black paper and prepare to assemble the caterpillar:

As a final touch, glue the yarn (cut in short half-inch segments) to the back of the body and head to make the caterpillar nicely fuzzy.

Display

During free time (or during another art period) have the children make some orange and/or yellow flowers. No formal instructions should be needed for this, even with very young children. The flowers should be of varied shapes and sizes, and will need leaves and stems of light green.

Cut some green leaves and staple them all along a four-foot length of green yarn to make a vine. Twine the vine around an empty wrapping paper tube which you've painted green and fasten it to the bulletin board with yarn and pins. Let it lean forward about eight inches at the top. (This is one display which really must be put on a bulletin board, since the parts will have to be secured with pins.) Now drape your snake around the vine with his head on the top and his tail trailing along the bottom. Arrange the flowers in random clumps (and if they won't all fit on the bulletin board, there's nothing wrong with utilizing the wall on both sides of it). Scatter the caterpillars among the flower groups; add some grass along the bottom edge and wherever else it seems to be needed.

Variation

Instead of having each child make a small caterpillar, have the entire class make one huge one. The procedure is essentially the same except that each child makes only one body segment and you make the face.

Young children especially enjoy designing wildly colored socks for their caterpillar segment. When the whole thing is assembled the overall effect is very amusing.

With a large class, two caterpillars could be made. Put them up facing each other on a long row of grass. Giant flowers could accompany the display and add to its color.

Chapter 6. Paper and Crayon Murals

Lesson 1
Lions and Palm Trees

Lions and Palm Trees

Preparation

These are large sitting-down pussy-cat lions and can be done in crayon or tempera. If crayon is used, encourage the children to color heavily and closely for best results.

Make some five-foot-tall palm trees. Cut up several whole sheets of newspapers for the leaves (want-ad sections or financial pages to obtain uniformity of grey color) and then tape a two-foot length of wire to the back of each. Newspaper is thin enough to permit you to cut at least three leaves at once.

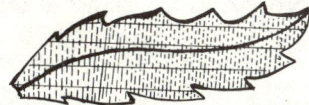

(Touch up the tips with green paint if you're more of a realist.)

Tape four cardboard egg cartons together end to end, (bumpy side out) and scrunch them together a bit in the center to make a nicely bending palm tree trunk.

Rescue the sun from the scarecrow display and pin it up at the side of the room; then tape your palm tree in front of it.

Now the scene is set for the lions.

Paper and Crayon Murals

Presentation

Pass out a 12″ × 18″ sheet of yellow or *light* brown construction paper to each child. They should draw in pencil with the paper placed vertically on their desks. Begin with the nose and jowls right in the middle of the paper:

Add eyebrow and eyes

and a tongue, and then draw an enclosing line around the entire face.

Add the mane (don't forget "bangs" at the forehead) and let the shaggy points of the mane swing out to the edges of the paper.

(Watch out that students do not make too many tiny points on the mane, or it will take forever to cut them out, and some frustration might occur.)

Now add a sitting down body and a paint-brush-type tail:

In the crayon application process, the only suggestions needed would be to color the white of the eyes with white and the pupils black. The iris can be any color the child choses; after the eyes are done, anything goes. If time is running out, (or if the ice is growing thin) the construction paper self color can be allowed to remain as is for the body or for parts of the face.

Display

After these beasts have been cut out and are safely identified on their backs by names and room numbers, furnish each child with a toothpick (for poking holes) and 6 to 10 broom straws for whiskers. Secure the whiskers with tape on the back and then put up the lions either to bask in the rays of the sun or in the shade of the sheltering palm.

Lesson 2
City Cats

City Cats

Preparation

Cut five pieces of grey and black paper (the 12" × 18" size) lengthwise to produce ten long rectangles. These are to be transformed into facsimiles of tall city buildings viewed at night and from a distance. You will also need to cut about 60 small yellow rectangles (1½" × 1") and 60 black ones. These are to be windows for the buildings: yellow for lighted ones and black for darkened ones.

During free moments, working either alone or in groups, the students can glue the windows on the buildings in rows. The yellow windows look best on the black paper, and the black windows look best on the grey. The buildings can be taped to the wall at varying heights as each is completed.

Make a fence to go in front of the building. (This will conceal the uneaven bases of the buildings and will also provide a display area for the cats which are to be made during the art period.) Fold five sheets of light brown paper accordian-pleat fashion. Do one section at a time so that you can angle-cut the tops to points when each piece of paper is still in the folded stage. Unfold the fence sections and draw on some wood grain lines with brown crayon (see method used for making trees described in chapter 7, lesson 3) if you like. Put up the fence in such a way as to preserve its semi-three-dimensional quality. Do this by allowing the fold lines to project out from the wall slightly. The setting, when completed, seems to be just waiting for some interesting little cats to come along.

Presentation

Pass out 9" × 12" paper and demonstrate how to draw the cat's body with the paper folded.

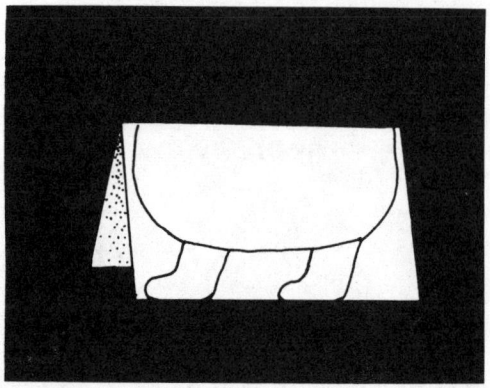

Keep the paper folded and cut out the body. A tail can be fashioned from the scraps which remain, and then glued in place. Set this aside to dry and begin to make the heads.

Each child will need a 4½" × 6" piece of paper in a color which matches his cat's body. An easy way to begin the face is to place the ears in the corners and then draw the shape of the face. Each child should use a crayon a shade darker than his paper for this part of the drawing.

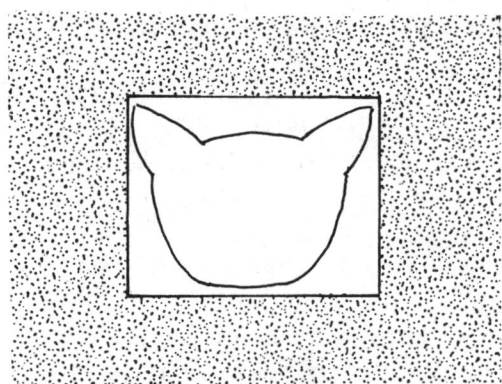

Add some shaggy points of fur between the ears and around the bottom of the face, and fill these in heavily with the crayon.

Then set in nose, eyes, and jowls with a black crayon. Be sure to slant the eyes toward the nose:

The whites of the eyes and the iris should be colored carefully so as not to smudge the black outline. A dot of white can be ground into one side of each iris to create a shiny effect.

Before the heads are glued in place, the bodies can be given a decorative treatment with the same crayon which was used to color the shaggy parts of the head.

Points of fur can be outlined on the body. Stripes, squiggles, spots or other designs can also be drawn and colored in. Each child will come up with something different and delightful.

When the bodies are finished, glue the heads in place. Tell the children to experiment with head positions and angles before deciding upon the final one. Each should choose the position which best suits the personality of his cat.

Paper and Crayon Murals

Display

Put up the cats along the top and bottom of the fence. They are most effective in groups; to achieve this some overlapping will be necessary.

For a final touch cut out a garbage can and lid from grey paper and let one little cat peep out from inside. The garbage can is an interesting spot for the display tag. Just print your grade and room number on it with a silver crayon.

Lesson 3
Elves and Mushrooms in Moonlight

Elves and Mushrooms in Moonlight

Preparation

Count out as many sheets of 9" × 12" construction paper as there are children in your class, plus one more for yourself. Use an assortment of bright colors but no neutrals (black, white, grey). Cut them in half on the paper cutter so as to obtain enough 6" × 9" pieces that each child may have two. Also, cut some light green paper into 4½" × 6" quarter sizes, one for each child.

Presentation

Put up a large, white, round moon (about twelve inches in diameter) in the front of your classroom. Explain that this is the beginning of a very bright and magical night in spring when colored mushrooms will rise from the ground and shy little elves will be popping up among them. These elves might look around and marvel at the new green growth and early hints of the summer that is to come.

If possible, and if you feel so inclined, play a recording of Debussy's "Clair de Lune," and then discuss the feelings and/or images evoked by the music. (Don't do it, however, if you believe that this would amount to an exploitation of Debussy.)

Invite each child to select two 6" × 9" pieces of paper in colors of high contrast. Demonstrate how to draw a mushroom stem and cap on one of the colors:

Cut out the cap and lay it on the second piece of paper, close to the bottom edge. Trace around the underside curve of the mushroom cap and then, after having removed the cap, make a corresponding convex curve from end to end:

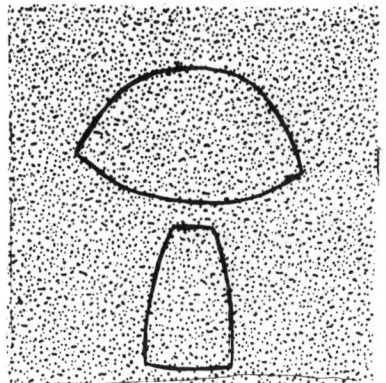

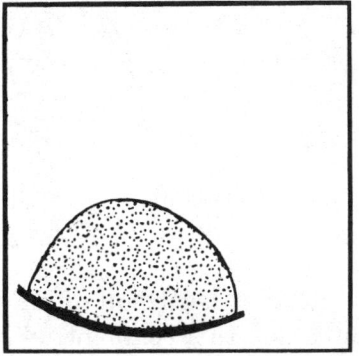

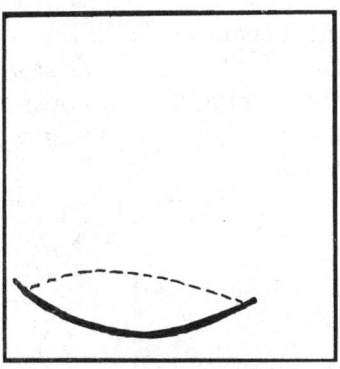

Glue it to the cap to create an underside look. Cut out the stem, glue it in place, and then make some lines with crayon which radiate from the top of the stem to the edge of the underside for a textural effect.

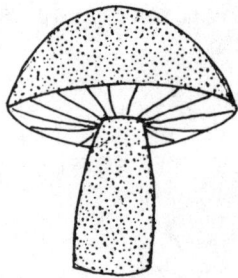

Cut some decorative spots out of the remaining mushroom paper. Glue them to the alternate piece of paper and cut them out again, leaving some of the second color to show around each. Glue the spots to the mushroom at random. Some might be cut in half to simulate the curvature of the cap.

Each child will have at least half of his second piece of paper left. He should now trade this remnant with a friend in order to obtain a new color (that is, a color he has not used anywhere in his mushroom so far). The new color will be used to make the elf. Begin with the shoulders: cut a hump that is just a bit smaller than the mushroom cap and glue it to the back of the mushroom. Pass out the light green paper and demonstrate ways to draw head and hands:

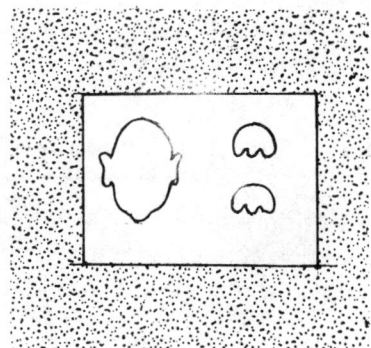

Glue these in place; add cap, hair and a surprised look on the elf's face, and he's ready to greet the spring.

Display

Cut about 14 hills from grey and black paper (two shades of the grey if you have it) and arrange them under the moon in overlapping clusters. Add some smaller rounded clumps of spring-green grass here and there. Several brightly colored free-form clouds around the white moon will give emphasis here, if you are putting this display on a white wall.

Put up the elves in groups among the hills. They almost arrange themselves, as you will discover.

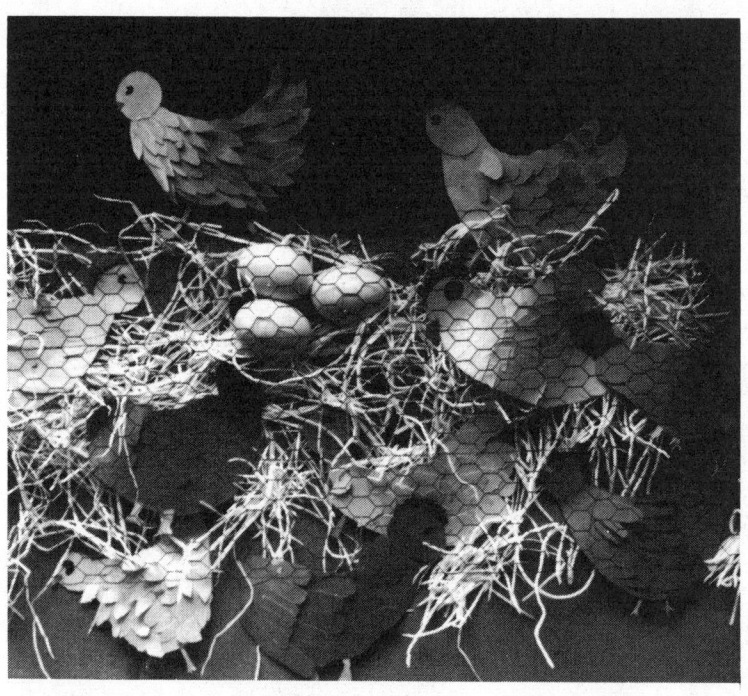

Lesson 4
Little Foxes
and Chickens

Little Foxes and Chickens

This is a rather long project and may easily be divided into two parts. The results are very good especially with second and third grade children.

Foxes

Preparation

From the supply room you will need one package each of 12" × 18" red and 9" × 12" white construction paper. Every child is supposed to get only one piece of each, but you may need some extras to compensate for mistakes. Cut some 9" × 12" black and green paper into quarters—one for each student.

Presentation

Pass out the paper and announce to the class that they will be making "red" foxes. You might get into some interesting discussions concerning the discrepancy between the color of the paper and real foxes' color. Once the issue is clarified, the figures should be started.

Begin by drawing the foxes' shoulders and feet at one end of the paper:

Cut this out, lay it in the middle of the paper and trace around the shoulder. Remove the piece and continue to make the thighs, back feet, head and tail.

After all pieces have been cut out, move on to the white paper. Lay the head on the white and draw lines from the nose to the ears

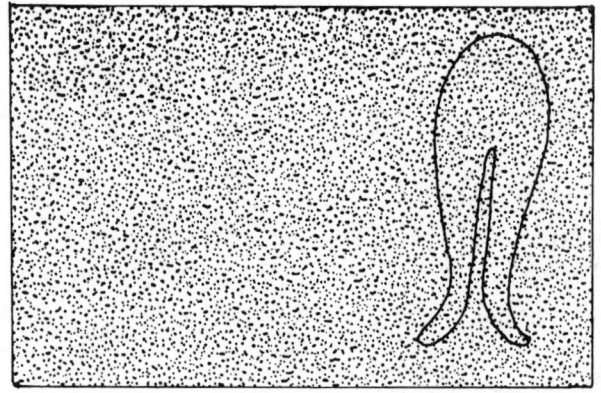

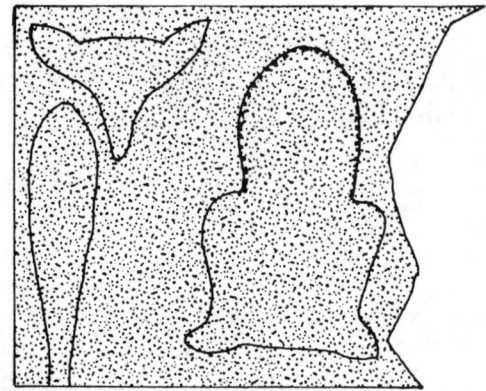

on each side of the face. Also draw an oval stomach and two football-shaped eyes:

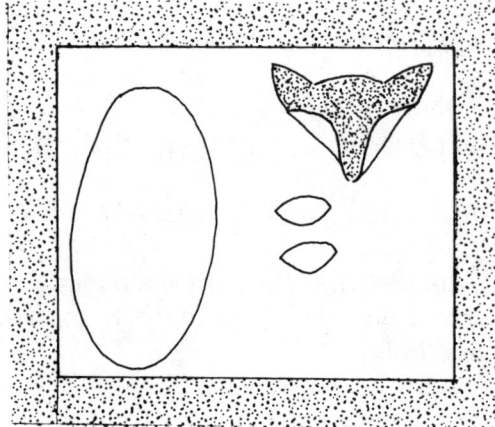

When all these parts have been cut out, glue the eyes to the black paper and cut out again, leaving a black edge all around. Glue green iris to the whites and put a black dot in the center with crayon.

Glue the red part of the head to the white part and then attach the eyes at a slant.

Next glue the white stomach oval to the large body section and fasten the shoulder-leg piece at the top. (This will allow the front legs to stand out a bit from the body and enable the fox to sit on the desk top for the rest of his construction.)

Glue the head in place after experimenting with various positions.

Finally, the tail should be frayed out a bit with small cuts all around the edge, before it is glued in place.

Display

Put up some rows of grass on one side of the bulletin board. Fasten the grass so that the foxes can be pushed into it a little way. Arrange the foxes in order of size, with the smallest ones on the top, until all have been displayed.

Hens

Preparation

The hens will require one large sheet (12″ × 18″) of either orange or yellow paper for each student.

Holding the paper lengthwise, draw a body, a head and about 24 feathers:

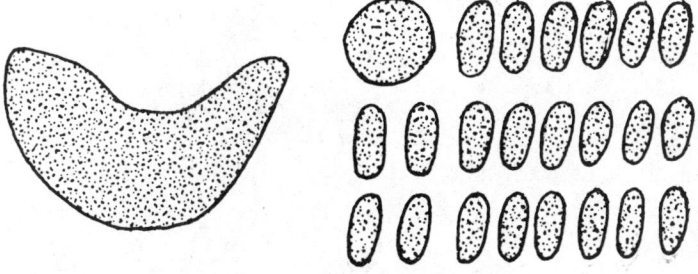

Of course, the feathers can be cut out several at a time by folding the paper to multiple thicknesses. Be sure, however, that the other parts have been cut out first so that the amount of paper left for the feathers has been definitely determined.

Glue the feathers to the body in rows which fan out slightly. Begin the first row at the tail and work toward the neck, overlapping the rows as you work foreward. The feathers should have only a small dab of glue at one end so that they can be pulled away from the body to give more texture.

When the feathers are all in place, add the head, comb, beak and eye. The children can trade leftover scraps with each other to make the legs and feet. That way, the yellow chickens will have orange feet and vice versa.

Display

On the remaining half of the bulletin board, beside the foxes, put up some straw or excelsior with straight pins. (White, stringy, plastic packing material looks good too.) Arrange the chickens at random in the straw, and tape in a few empty egg-shaped hosiery containers for interest. Cover the hen side of the bulletin board with several feet of chicken wire. (You may have to secure this with nails at each end of the wire, but it's worth doing since it will hold everything else in place.)

In back of the chickens and foxes, put up some black hills topped by silhouettes of farm buildings. A big white moon plus some clouds will finish the sky, and one lone far-away fox seen in front of the moon adds a final touch.

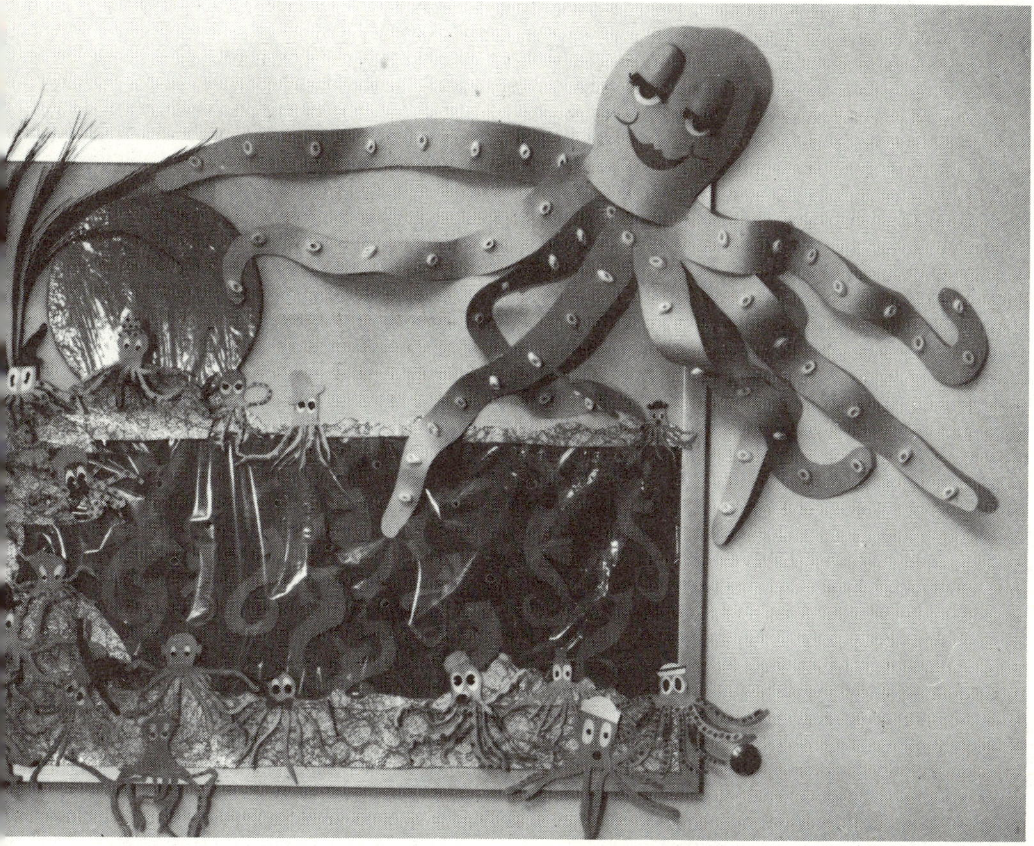

Lesson 5
Seahorses
and Octopuses
_____

Seahorses and Octopuses

This project is similar to the last in its organization: Two different (but related) products will be used in a final display, so you might want to present it in several separate art sessions.

Octopuses

Preparation

Make a large octopus from a light shade of pink paper. Cut the head out of one piece of 9" × 12" stock, and utilize as much of this space as you can. Then cut eight tentacle pieces from 12" × 18" paper. (Make a stack of four sheets so that you will actually be cutting sixteen segments. These, when glued together, will yield eight units of two segments each.)

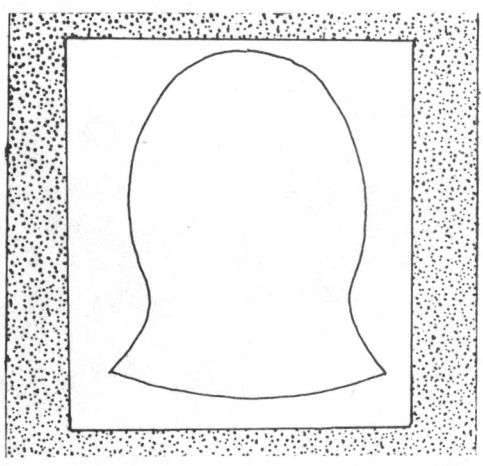

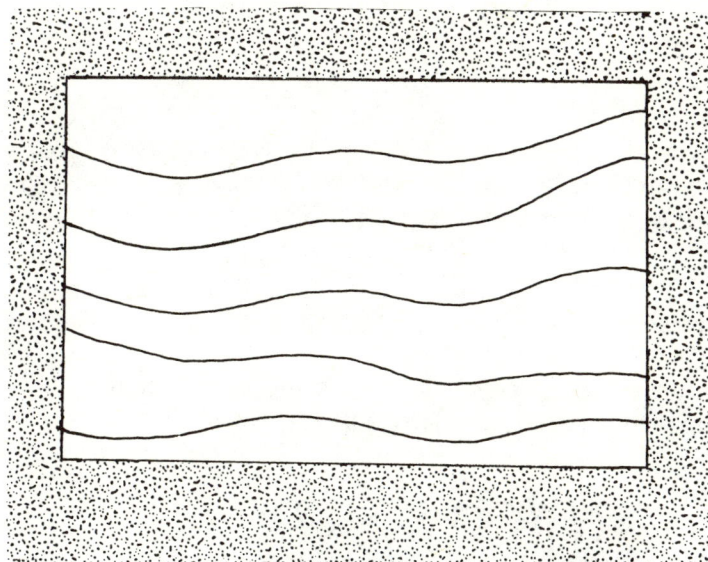

Taper the end of each tentacle after assembling.

Finish the head by gluing on eyes, eyelids with curled lashes, and a cut-paper smile. Then arrange and attach the eight tentacles. These can be further embellished with plastic (packing pieces) suction cups. If you lack that material, simply make circles with crayon along each tentacle.

Presentation

Put up the giant octopus above the bulletin board. Arrange the arms so that they encircle the space within. Explain to your class that this is a mother octopus who has brought her babies out on the rocks for some sun. The babies will be made in the same way as the mother was, but they will be much smaller.

Pass out 9" × 12" pink construction paper and let the students discover how best to make the baby octopuses. When the bodies have been completed and all eight legs have been glued in position, some may like the idea of gluing ticket punch circles along the tentacles to represent suction cups. This effect could also be achieved by drawing the circles with crayon. Put out the scrap boxes so that the octopuses may be finished with eyes, nose, mouth and other interesting additions such as hats, collars, ties, gloves, etc.

Seahorses

Preparation

The seahorses will require two contrasting colors of paper such as yellow and orange. Half of a 9" × 12" sheet of each of the two colors will be plenty for each child.

Explain to the class that they will be making some seahorses—playmates for the baby octopuses. They will turn out to be about the same size but quite different and more complicated in form.

Put this drawing on the board, and present it just as you would a diagram for a cursive writing lesson.

Since this is to be the back of the drawing (thus eliminating pencil lines) it might be a good idea to have each child print his name before cutting out the form. Place the cut out form on the yellow paper and trace all around it from the neck down. Before cutting this out, make a new curved dotted line from neck to tail. Then cut on the dotted line.

Turn both pieces over so that name and pencil lines are on the back and glue the yellow part on top of the orange.

Place this assembled piece on top of the remaining yellow paper and draw and cut the fanned headpiece (which children love to exaggerate in size) and the fin.

Paper and Crayon Murals 165

Add the white circles and (wedge-removed) black circles for the eyes, and the seahorses are complete.

Display

Cover the entire bulletin board with one color of construction paper. Orange is a good choice. Arrange a row of crinkled foil-paper rocks across the middle. (These can be made of wrapping paper salvaged from Christmas presents or, lacking that, used crumpled finger-paint paper. (The idea is to make the rocks look shiny and wet.)

Arrange the seahorses in the area between the rocks and the bottom of the bulletin board, overlapping where necessary so that all can be included. Cover the lower half of the bulletin board (and the seahorses) with a long piece of cellophane to represent the water in which they are swimming. Then add some more rock-piles at the bottom of the bulletin board. Cluster them so as to define the shape of the pool.

The baby octopuses go on the rocks, and, if you run out of space, put some of them on the bulletin board frame itself or even outside it. Balance the display by placing a cellophane sun in the sky and by adding several clusters of weeds for texture.

This bulletin board is an especially effective stimulus for a creative writing lesson. The characters displayed could be construed as a projective technique and viewed accordingly. Stories which may result from the combination of mother and baby octopuses plus seahorses should be well worth reviewing. (Be prepared, also, for that child who will single out the alternate plural spelling: *octopi*.)

Lesson 6
Sit-Down People _____

Sit-Down People

Preparation

Accordion-pleat three pieces of 12" x 18" construction paper. These are the beginnings of a grandstand which will hold the paper spectators your class is going to make. Next, fold three pieces of 12" × 18" cardboard into L shapes and staple the accordion-pleated sections to them at top and bottom:

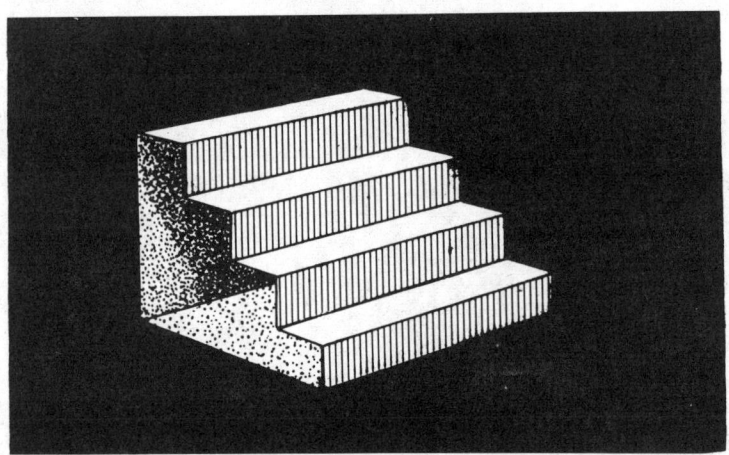

Place the grandstand sections side by side on your desk. If the seats have a tendency to sag a bit, reinforce them by stuffing crumpled paper into the hollow.

Presentation

After the students have viewed the grandstand and have some

idea of the scale involved, they can start immediately to make the people. Pass out sheets of 6″ × 9″ pink construction paper, and put a guideline sketch on the board. Begin with a circle for the head and then continue to draw a simple symmetrical human form.

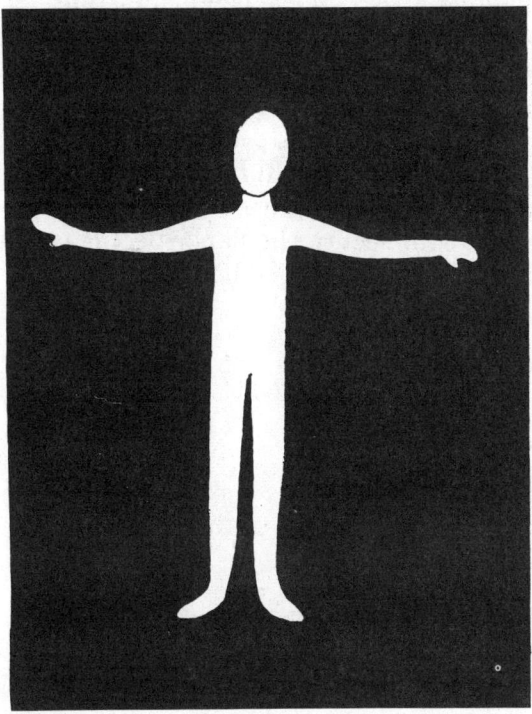

The main purpose here is to make the basic drawing as easy as possible so that early success will motivate innovations during the completion of the project.

After the basic figures have been cut out, they should be bent experimentally until a convincing sitting position has been achieved, and then shortened or lengthened to fit the stadium seats.

Each student should decide privately the kind of sports event his or her person is watching. (The inconsistencies which will result rather amplify the interest of the final display.) Each child should then set about clothing the spectator appropriately, using paper from the scrap boxes.

You might need to have on hand some special materials to fill individual requests such as: toothpicks (pennant staffs), cellophane (sunglasses), foil stars (daredevil fans), and tape (emergencies).

Paper and Crayon Murals

Display

Put up a row of buildings such as those used in the "City Cats" display (Chapter 6, lesson 2), and then pin the stadium securely in front of the buildings. A white fence made from narrow strips of paper should go in front of the stadium and extend around the sides. This can be secured with tape at the corners and with pins at the back.

The children can seat their people wherever they seem to fit best. However, some care should be taken in these placements to avoid canceling the smaller figures. When the final arrangement has been agreed upon, secure the paper people to their seats with small circles of masking tape. (Too bad you can't do that to the real ones sometimes!)

Chapter 7. Dynamic Figures

Lesson 1
Running and Jumping Scarecrows

Running and Jumping Scarecrows

Preparation

Each child will need two harmonious colors of 9″ × 12″ construction paper (e.g., orange and yellow, purple and pink, dark blue and light blue, turquoise and chartreuse). Cut enough 2″ × 2″ pieces of pink and the same number of 4″ × 4″ yellow. One piece 12″ × 18″ black construction paper for each child will also be needed.

For your presentation, make a big yellow paper sun with lots of emanating rays, and cut some tiny green plant sprouts from light green and display them temporarily.

Presentation

Explain to the children that one function of a scarecrow is to deceive the birds and thereby discourage them from eating or disturbing newly planted spring seedbeds. Their job is done when the seeds have successfully sprouted. So when green plantlets appear, a wild, scarecrow spring celebration dance can easily be imagined.

To make the scarecrows, fold one of the 9″ × 12″ colored papers the long way and show on the board how to draw the shirt:

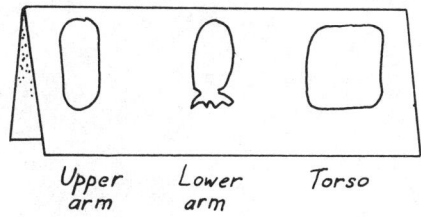

Dynamic Figures

Keep the paper folded to cut out the first two sections (upper arms and lower arms), and unfold to cut out the large torso section.

Fold the other color of construction paper and draw the overalls sections.

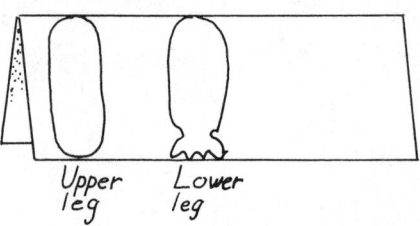

To draw the torso, take the torso section from the shirt and trace around it exactly:

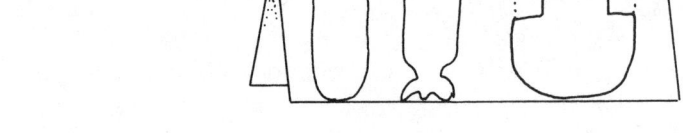

Then make indentations for the shoulder straps.

Cut out the overall pieces and glue the overall torso piece to the blouse torso piece immediately. Spread out everything neatly:

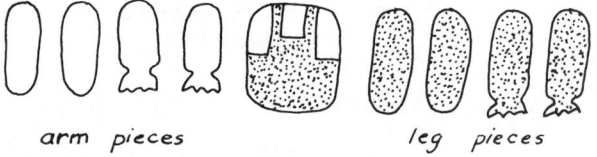

Everybody will have four arm pieces, four leg pieces and the one combined torso piece.

Use circles of masking tape on the backs of *your* pieces to show the class how the scarecrow can achieve all degrees of animation simply by joining the pieces at anatomical joint places.

Dynamic Figures

The children should be allowed ample time to experiment with the various jumping and running positions. They'll be noisy, so be sure to close your door. (If you're *really* brave, put Stravinsky's "Rite of Spring" on the record player and let the children be the scarecrows for awhile—but that takes *courage*, particularly if it's on a Friday!)

When all the activity has subsided, the children can glue their figures into a final position.

Round heads and necks should be cut next from the pink paper and then glued to the bodies.

The yellow paper is for straw which will be emerging from the ends of the blouse and legs (real straw or a collection of dried grass is better.)

The hat can be made from a piece of 2" × 3" brown paper—*or* from jute carpet padding, if you've managed to build your salvage material scrap collection that far.

With a bit of colored fabric (or red paper) for a neck scarf, the figure is ready to be glued in its entirety to the 12" × 18" black paper.

Here is one of the best tricks you can know: Explain that the scarecrows should be cut out (after having been glued to the black paper) with a quarter inch of edging sticking out all around. This emphasizes the animation and pulls the entire form together. It also makes the figures stand out from the background.

With the leftover time (?) and leftover black paper scraps, children can fashion eyes and noses:

Dynamic Figures

Display

Put up your sun and sprouting green plants (these should also be black-edged to match the scarecrows), then display the cavorting scarecrows among them.

If you want to go further, have the children make some crows to go with the display

and some spring-sky colored clouds to catch the shortest rays of the sun.

Lesson 2
Raincoated Puddle-Jumpers

Raincoated Puddle-Jumpers

Preparation

Cut a 3" × 5" rectangle of fabric (as many different patterns as you can find) for each child in your room. These will later be cut into colorful umbrellas by the children. Everyone will also need a piece of 6" × 9" yellow construction paper (for raincoats), a popsicle stick (for the umbrella handle) 4½" × 6" piece of black (for boots), a square inch of white, and a full 9" × 12" sheet of black for assembly and backing.

Cut some blue cellophane into puddle shapes

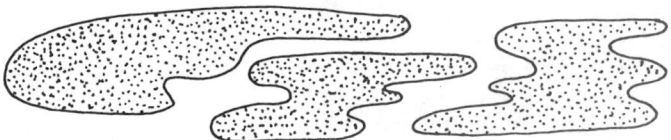

and about 30 raindrop shapes from the blue cellophane scraps.

When you're alone, practice reading aloud a poem on rainwear such as A. A. Milne's "Happiness."

Presentation

Pass out materials and read the poem to the children. Get good trudging cadence to it as you read. The children will empathize with John walking through nicely sloppy puddles on a drippy April day.

The class should make the umbrellas first (from the fabric). Put a drawing of an umbrella on the board and let the children copy it (in pencil) on the fabric; then cut it out. (N.B.: If your class is a very early primary grade, these umbrellas should be pre-cut by teenage "helpers" before the project is begun. Little fingers have difficulties in cutting fabric and frustrations may occur.)

After the umbrella shapes are set aside, the hat and raincoat shapes should be directed and cut from the yellow paper. (The hat stays connected to the raincoat during the cutting-out phase.)

Place the umbrellas, handles (popsicle sticks) and raincoats on the large sheet of black paper. After a satisfactory relationship of parts has been achieved, everything should be glued down and allowed to dry. Meanwhile the boots can be made and cut out from the small extra piece of black paper.

Cut out the umbrella-holding figures, allowing an outline edging of the black paper to show all around.

Attach the black boots on the back.

Dynamic Figures

Display

Put up some blue-edged white clouds and then string the cellophane raindrops on yarn so that they slant down to the cellophane puddles.

Arrange the figures in and between the puddles.

Lesson 3
Elves At Work

Elves at Work

A variety of accomplishments have been attributed to elves, and one of the most traditional is that of painting leaves in the fall. This activity, as depicted by children, makes a truly spectacular display.

Preparation

Leaves

Provide each child with a piece of 9" × 12" construction paper—white or any light color. Put a simple leaf shape on the board and suggest that the students use it as a guide to create their own leaf shapes on the paper. Attach a short stem to the leaf, and suggest ways that the space might be broken up inside the shape.

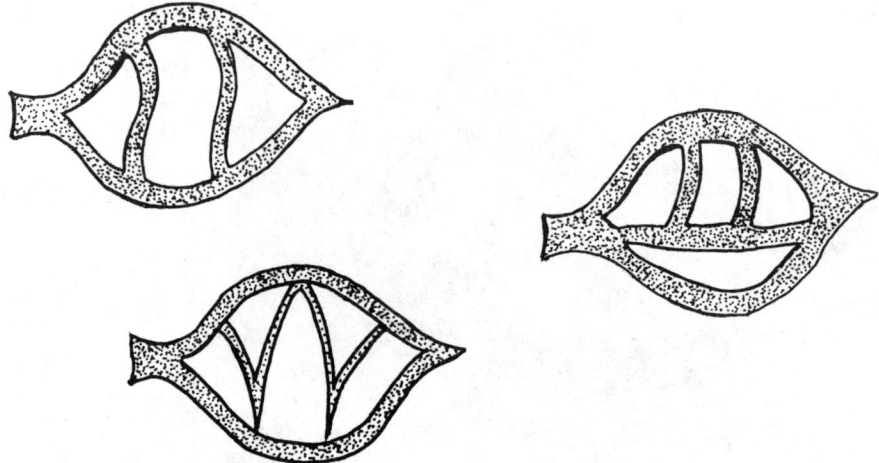

Designs can then be added, keeping in mind that the leaves are supposedly being painted by imaginary individuals, and that the designs should reflect this.

The best medium for coloring the leaves is crayon, heavily applied, in warm colors (red, magenta, pink, yellow and orange). After the coloring process is completed, cut them out and apply accents of gold glitter (if you have any) for emphasis.

Elves

Before beginning to draw the elves, direct each child to imagine himself in a leaf-painting position and then experiment with several poses. The elves will be about the same size as the leaves, so a half sheet of 9″ × 12″ construction paper will be enough to begin to make each suit. The suit might consist of a jacket-plus-trousers ensemble cut from several colors, or a unified costume cut from just one:

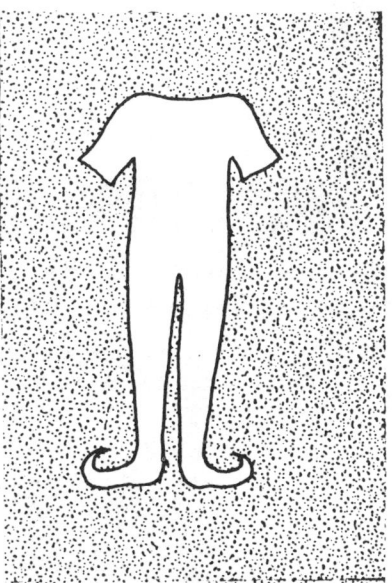

Supply a variety of pastel colors so that choices may be made for cutting out heads, hands and feet. Facial features may be drawn in crayon or pen, or manufactured by cutting the forms from additional bits of colored construction paper found in the scrap box. Accessories, too can be fashioned from scraps. As the elves are finished, they should be backed with black and cut out, leaving an edge, as described in earlier lessons.

Dynamic Figures

Display

You will need to make an almost life-sized tree to contain the leaves and elves. One of the most rewarding aspects of the project lies in the fact that this part will require only seven 12″ × 18″ sheets of light brown paper for its construction. Lay out three of the sheets horizontally and, using a yellow crayon, draw several ovals spaced at random on each piece of paper:

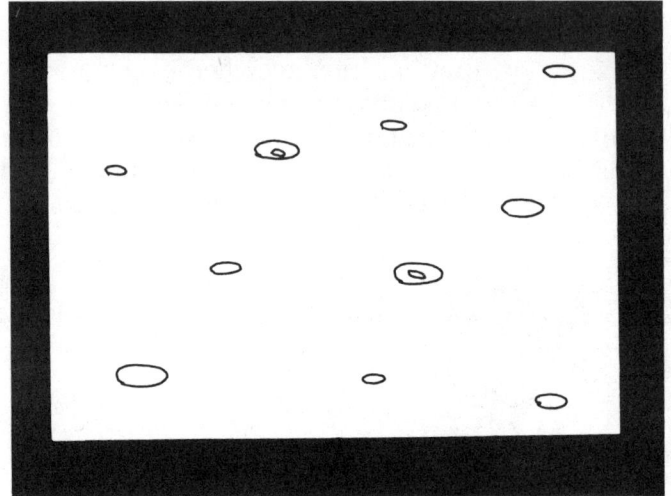

Make parallel wood-graining lines around the ovals; be sure to press down hard on the crayon as you work:

On the remaining four pieces of paper make some limbs and give them the same wood-graining treatment:

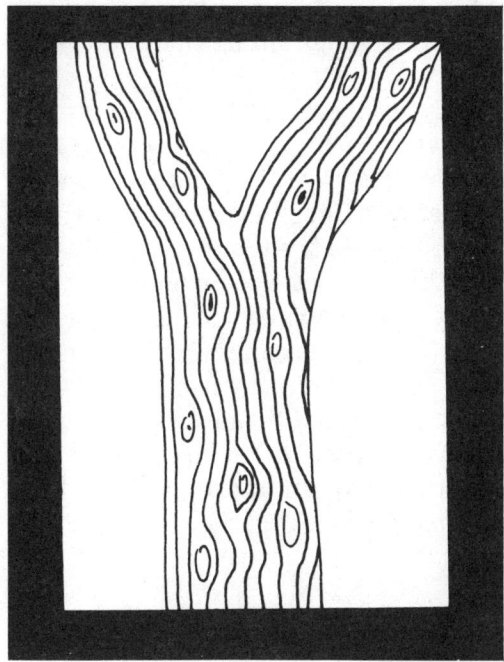

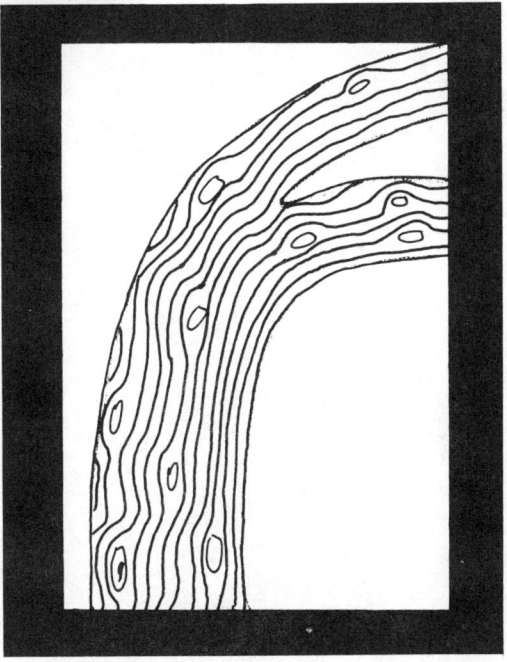

Mix a quarter of a cup of brown tempera paint with an equal quantity of water. Brush it directly over the crayon work on all units of brown paper. The paint will roll off the waxy crayon lines but will be absorbed by the paper, thus heightening the wood grain look.

When the paper is thoroughly dry, cut out the limb sections and begin to tape the tree to the wall. You will need a space 8 feet high and 6 feet wide for this display. Begin at the floor with one of the trunk sections. Tape it so that it bulges outward for a semi-three-dimensional effect. Continue to build the trunk vertically one section at a time until all three of the units have been used. Let the limbs and branches "grow" out of the top and sides of the trunk in a gracefully balanced arrangement. The leaves can then be arranged at the ends of the branches so that they point away from the trunk.

The elves with their paint buckets, brushes and ladders can be taped in place by the children. Each student, understanding the posture and function of his elf, will make an appropriate and interesting placement which will finally work together as a unit.

Lesson 4
Balloonists in Berry Baskets

Balloonist in Berry Baskets

Preparation

Save plastic berry baskets until you have one for every two children; then cut two whole sides out of each:

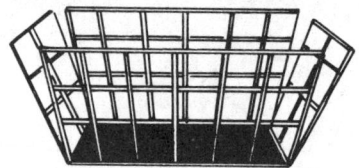

You will also need an assortment of colored yarn (a four-foot segment for each student), five or six jars of tempera, 9" × 12" construction paper, and 12" × 18" sky blue paper.

Presentation

Pass out the 9" × 12" sheets and announce that this paper will be converted into a picture of an ascending balloon. You may want to develop a discussion around the subject of man's early attempts at flight and the invention of the balloon. The subject appeals strongly to children of all ages.

Fold a piece of notebook paper in half lengthwise; then draw a balloon shape and cut it out.

Unfold the shape and trace around it on the construction paper.

Refold the balloon and cut a curved slice from the outside.

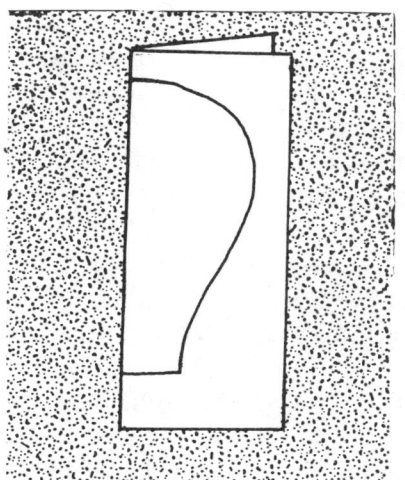 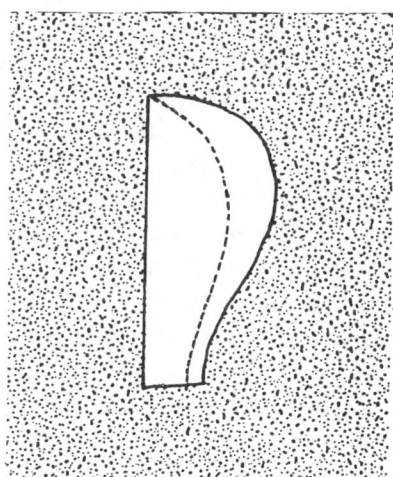

Unfold the altered shape, center it on the construction paper, and draw around it again. Repeat the process. The final balloon drawing on the construction paper will have five contoured symmetrical stripes to be painted alternately.

While the balloons are being cut out, pass out the 12″ × 18″ sky blue paper and the basket pieces. The balloon is to be glued close to the top of the blue. The placement of the basket will define the

Dynamic Figures

height of the balloonist, since he will have to fit inside the space between the basket and balloon. When that space has been determined, the baskets should be glued in place and then the entire composition set aside to dry undisturbed.

Now the balloonist can be made from scrapbox material. A simple pair of trousers and matching jacket make easy starting points. The legs may be straight since the balloonist is standing in a rather confining area, but arms could be bent to give the figure more interest. Boots, mittens, helmet (with ticket-punch goggles) and a flying scarf might be suggested as the figure construction progresses.

Place the figures as far down in the basket as they will go and then glue them to the blue paper. Attach the yarn with glue along the stripes of the balloon and then tie each segment to the basket.

Cut out the entire unit so that the only blue showing will be behind the basket and the balloonist:

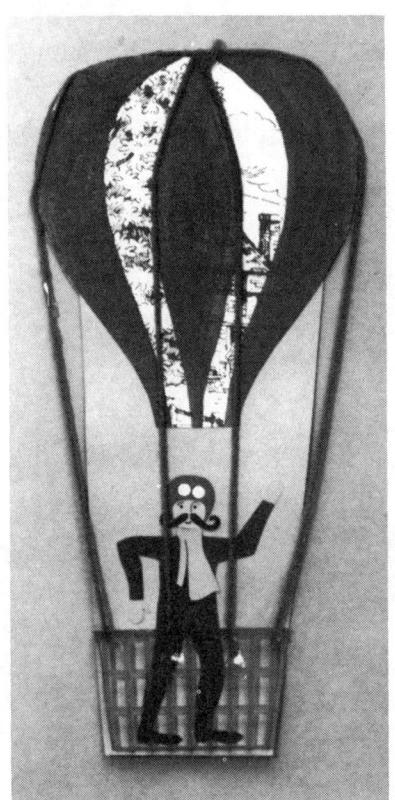

They are cut out in this way so that all the balloons will appear to be separately suspended units when they are assembled in the display.

Display

Stack 8 sheets of 12″ × 18″ construction paper. Use as many different shades of green as you can find—four if possible. Cut the sheets at an 80-degree angle from the corner.

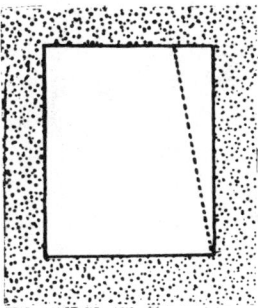

These are to represent fields shown in perspective as if viewed from the air. Tape four of them to the wall side by side, overlapping at the bottom, to achieve this effect.

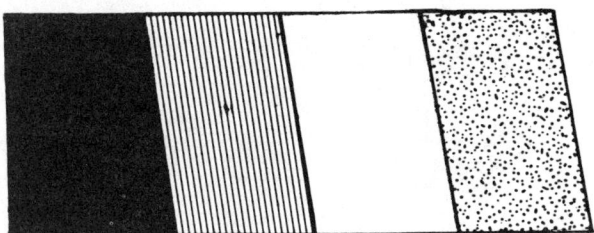

Then flip the remaining 4 pieces of paper over to reverse the direction, and finish the fields the other way.

This entire section should be started on a wall about a foot from the floor, so that the viewer's eye level will be well above it.

Start to put up the sky exactly at the top of the fields. Use the same color of blue that the students have used for backing paper. Twelve sheets of this (positioned horizontally) should complete enough sky to accommodate all of the balloons.

Stack eight more sheets of green paper of the same shades you've used for the fields. Cut out some low rolling mountains; then alternate and overlap them along the horizon line.

Make a very tiny sign about two inches square for the display tag such as: "BALLOON RACE TODAY—GRADE__." Tape it to the lower left field. About midway up that field, put up another sign (twice the size as the first) which says: "START." The "FINISH" sign may be posted on the ground close to the horizon line, or may be suspended between two balloons hovering there.

Hang the first several balloons as low as possible. The basket parts can be shown against a mountain but the upper parts (from the basket railing on up) should be placed against the sky color. Work upward until all the balloons are displayed. There is no reason why some of them can't be floating right out of the picture toward the ceiling.

Lesson 5
Walnut-Head People

Walnut-Head People

Preparation

Ask all your friends and neighbors to save half-shells from English walnuts for you. When you have collected enough for the class, it's time to begin.

Presentation

Announce to your students that they will be making some really "nutty" people. The heads are to be walnut shells and the costumes will come from the fabric scrap box. Since these figures will reflect unusual personalities, take a few minutes to discuss who they might be.

Begin the bodies in much the same way as you did the scarecrows in the first lesson of this chapter. Pass out 9" × 12" pink paper to everyone. This is then folded lengthwise and the following parts drawn on it.

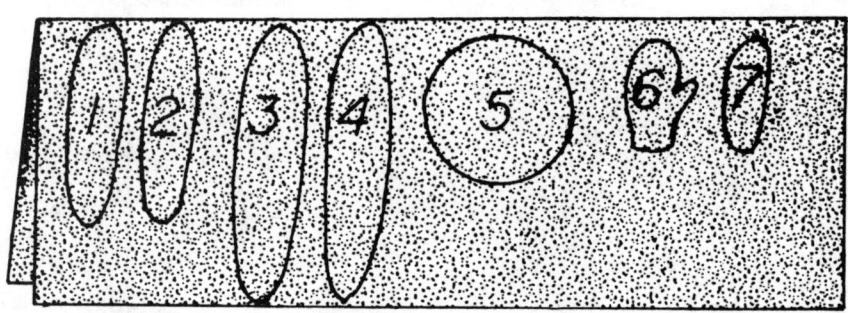

Number the parts as shown in the diagram. As they are cut out (two of each, since the paper is kept folded) the duplicate parts should also be numbered. To simplify assembly, direct the children to line up everything on their desks in sequence:

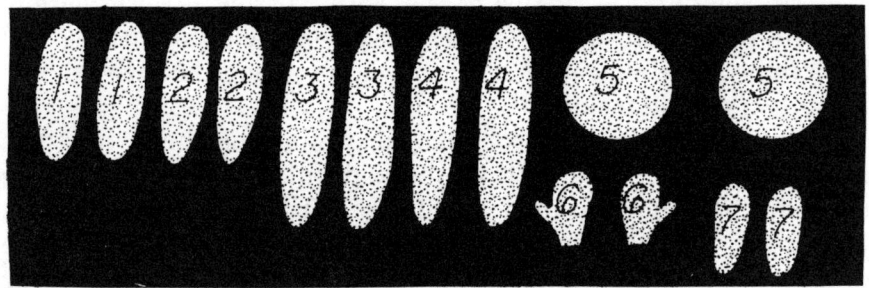

Working on a larger scale, you should do the same thing in front of the class, attaching your numbered pieces to the chalkboard with circles of tape.

Begin with the two number 5 pieces and overlap them slightly. This makes the torso. Next attach the number 1's at the top of the torso to define the shoulder and upper arms. Continue to assemble the figure until it is complete except for the head:

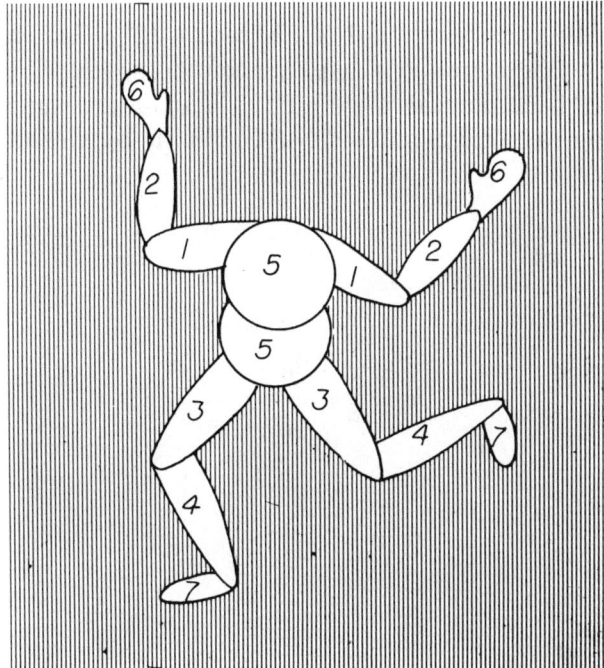

Dynamic Figures

Experiment with several different positions before the final gluing. Be sure to bend the joints for more action. When the figures are finished this far, each student will have a sort of paper doll to outfit with a set of clothes.

To facilitate the cutting of the cloth, borrow several pairs of large desk scissors from the other teachers. A lot of cutting will have to be done, so while half of the class is using the scissors, the other half can be making the heads.

Facial features are most easily drawn on the shell with India ink and then filled in with tempera paint. The eyes should be shaped first and then filled in entirely with white. While that is drying the other features can be finished. Last of all, the iris of the eyes can be painted directly on to the whites. Yarn, twine, rope, or string can be converted into hair of unusual interest and attached with glue.

Each student should assemble his figure on a piece of 9" × 12" colored paper of his own choosing. Shoes, gloves, hats and any other accessories may be added at this time to complete the characterization of the figure.

Display

The pictures should be matted on 12" × 15" paper in individual contrasting colors. To display the pieces, simply tape them to the wall in a random arrangement. Children are usually amused by a display tag which reads: "Nutty People by Grade___."

Lesson 6
Humpty-Dumpties

Multiple Humpty Dumpties

This is a good project for early spring when rabbits and colored eggs seem impossibly far away; (and spring vacation too!) Make Humpty Dumpties fills the void nicely and gives everyone hope that Easter is coming.

Preparation

Make a five-foot-long paper wall (about 9 inches high) by gluing pieces of white paper together in a length or else use shelf paper cut to half its width. Draw random free-form stones on the paper with black marker.

You will need to make patterns for the children to use in cutting their egg shapes. That's right, *patterns*! See opposite page. (All the Humpty Dumpties should be the same size, and for that reason, the use of a pattern is justified. The creativity of the student is sufficiently challenged and developed later in the project; why risk loss of enthusiasm on the part of a child who is unable to draw a satisfactory egg shape?)

Get out your paper scrap boxes and your most interesting collections of appealing miniscule junk such as carpeting scraps, fabric, jewelry, vinyl, foil, sequins, yarn, thread, feathers, wall-

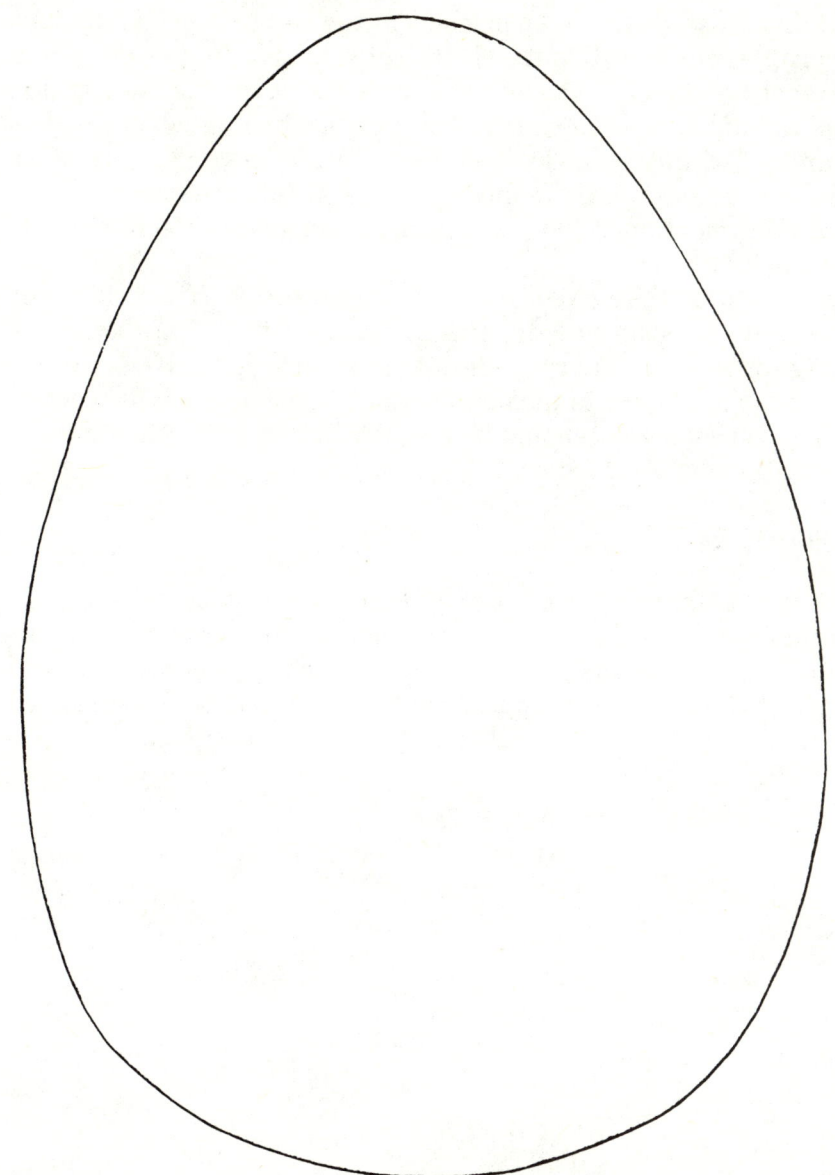

paper, dried weeds, seeds and grains, pasta, cellophane bits, and buttons.

Presentation

Put up your wall at the front of the room with masking tape,

Dynamic Figures

and invite associative responses from the children. You may have to drop some broad hints about eggs to get to the subject of "Humpty Dumpty." At any rate, once the poem has been recited you can introduce the idea that no one knows what the *real* Humpty Dumpty looks like because he is an imaginary character. You can suggest various modes of dress, but the assortment of materials mentioned earlier will motivate more effectively than words.

Pass out white paper and the egg patterns. When each child has the basic shape ready, the contents of the scrap boxes and collage should be explored. Allow a double art period here. It takes a great deal of time to make important decisions such as whether orange carpet scraps should be used for hair or boots should be cut from plastic or flint paper.

Display

Put up the wall at its display location and poke several handfuls of twigs behind it. This creates the effect of a forest behind the wall. Blue cloud shapes behind the trees adds an early-spring feeling. Put the Humpty Dumpties on the wall, behind the trees, and even in the trees. A cornball title for the display might be:

```
       WILL THE REAL
       HUMPTY DUMPTY
          PLEASE
           FALL
           DOWN?
```

Lesson 7
Sailors on a Yacht

Sailors on a Yacht

Preparation

Draw a large simplified version of a yacht on the chalkboard. It should be about two feet high and six feet long:

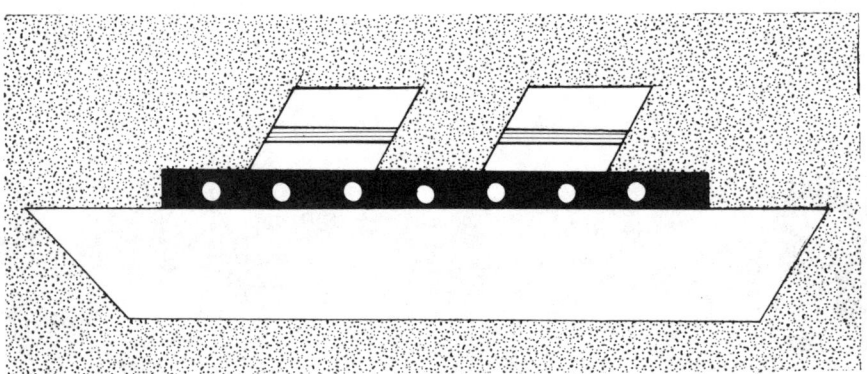

Now set about constructing a paper sailor to stand on the deck of the chalk line boat. Make his uniform in two pieces on a half sheet of blue paper.

Cut a head and neck from a small bit of pink paper. From a 4½" × 6" piece of white you can cut hands, eyes (use a ticket punch), shoes and a hat (measured to fit the head). Fold the paper and cut two of everything.

Assemble the sailor by first gluing the jacket to the trousers in an overlapped position; then place the head and neck section in back of the V neck so that the skin color will show through the opening. Add a dot of black to the eye centers and draw a smiling

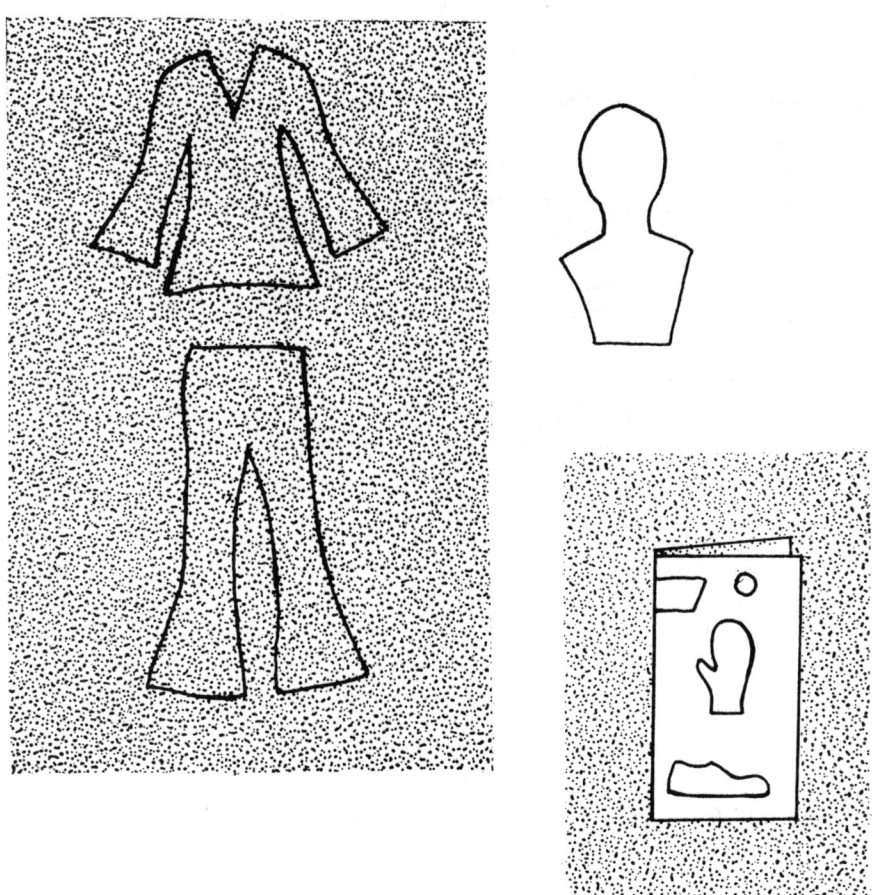

mouth on the face. As the final touch, tie a knot in the center of a four inch strip of colored fabric (red is good) and glue it to the bottom of the neck opening.

Presentation

Tape your sailor to the deck of the chalkboard boat.

Point out to the class that there is enough deck space left to accommodate an entire crew, and that when all the sailors are finished and standing in their places, an imaginary voyage can be planned.

Direct the students to make their sailors just as you did yours. Many individual size differences will occur, and these contrasts add interest when the display is completed.

Dynamic Figures

Display

Some of the children who finish early might want to start to work on the boat. It could be made of grey construction paper with black smokestacks and a white railing. The chalkboard boat can serve as a blueprint, but students will want to contribute detail ideas of their own. When the boat is finished, put it on the wall with plenty of tape (it will be heavy). Several clouds can be added in the background, plus enough wavy blue water in front to float the boat.

Tape the sailors in position so that they stand behind the railing all across the deck. Fold each right arm upwards in a saluting position, and then start planning the trip!

Lesson 8
Dancing Skeletons

Dancing Skeletons

This is simple and fast, and a good way to help students overcome the I-can't-draw-people syndrome.

Preparation

If your students haven't yet brought you quantities of that white spaghetti-like plastic stuff used for packing breakables, then get some yourself from any gift store (they're pleased to give it away!) Besides this material, all you need is black paper and glue to make dancing skeletons.

Presentation

A good place to begin this skeleton is at the shoulders and rib cage. Put a drawing on the chalkboard (using the chalk on its side for wider lines) and explain that each chalk line represents one piece of the plastic. Start with a horizontal line for the shoulders, and off each end of this, make the upper arms—two lines for each.

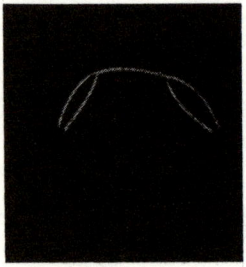

Join the lower arms to the uppers and bend at the elbow joint.

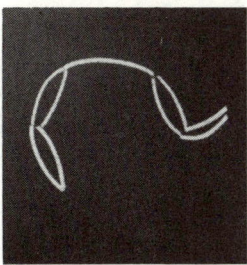

Add the ribcage and pelvis and then go on to the legs. The legs should be composed of longer segments than the arms. They should also bend at the joints.

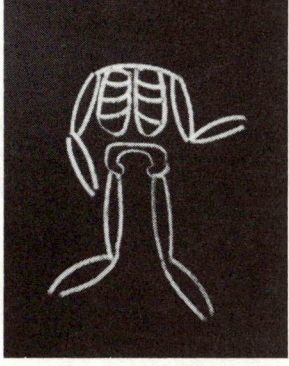

Hands and feet are five straight lines each, and the head, or skull, is a simple inverted pear shape.

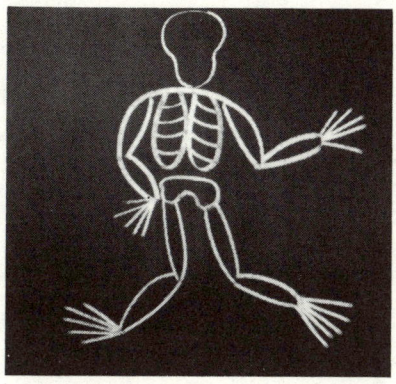

Dynamic Figures

After your drawing has been completed, the students should feel ready to attempt their skeleton figure compositions. Pass out 9" × 12" black paper and handfuls of the plastic material.

Each child can arrange his pieces as he wishes by using the chalkboard drawing as a guide, or by experimenting and then executing his own ideas about skeleton structure. The more the limbs are bent at the joints, the more action the figure will demonstrate.

Skulls can be formed from plastic discs (another variety of packing material) or simply cut from white construction paper. Give each child two black ticket-punched circles for eyes. When the arrangement is complete, the pieces should be glued in place and left undisturbed for at least 30 minutes.

Display

Each picture can be mounted separately on orange or yellow paper and then arranged at random on a wall—or they can be tacked on a bulletin board which has been covered with orange paper. You can use some of the plastic to spell out your grade and room number on black paper, and then tack it up along with the display.

Lesson 9
Silhouettes Go to a Picnic

Silhouettes Go to a Picnic

Preparation

A figure-drawing method much like that described earlier in this chapter (lesson 5) will be used here. However, for this project, pencil lines will function as the cut-paper forms had before. No preparation is necessary except to have on hand a package of 9″ × 12″ black construction paper.

Presentation

After the paper has been distributed, the students should practice drawing people in action. Demonstrate on the chalkboard that the figure starts with two overlapping circles which will represent the body's torso. Connect two long ovals as arm segments at the top of the upper circle, where the shoulders would be:

Add two more arm segments (those between the elbow and wrist) and allow them to form angles where they join:

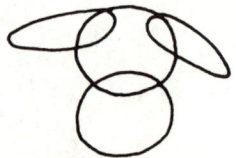

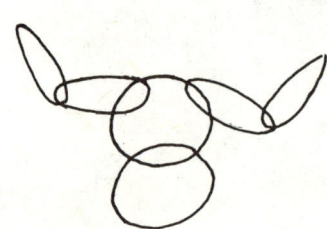

Dynamic Figures

Use slightly larger ovals to draw the legs. The first two segments join the lower torso section in such a way as to keep continuity of the form, so start to draw these ovals from the inside of the circle:

Again, create angles at the knee joints to express action:

Dynamic Figures

To complete this rough-in, add a neck and head, plus small ovals for hands and larger ones for feet:

Many adjustments may be necessary before each student achieves a well-proportioned figure. All of the work should be done on one side of the paper only, so that the other side is free from pencil marks.

Explain that each figure will be a silhouette, a kind of "shadow picture" in which only edge details can be seen, and any lines or forms in the middle will not show in the finished product. These silhouettes will depict people enjoying picnic activities in a park, late in the day. Body action and clothing should be geared to anything that might happen at a picnic. Softball, badminton, volley ball, hide-and-seek, jumping rope, tree climbing, sack racing and bicycling are some of the alternatives with which to start.

The clothes should be added as a contoured outline to the form of the body.

Fabric weight can be accounted for by showing how it is affected by the body's activity. Hair outline, hats and sports equipment will complete the drawing phase of the project, and then everything will be ready to cut out.

To determine which are the final cutting lines and hopefully avoid mistakes, it might be wise to trace around the complete

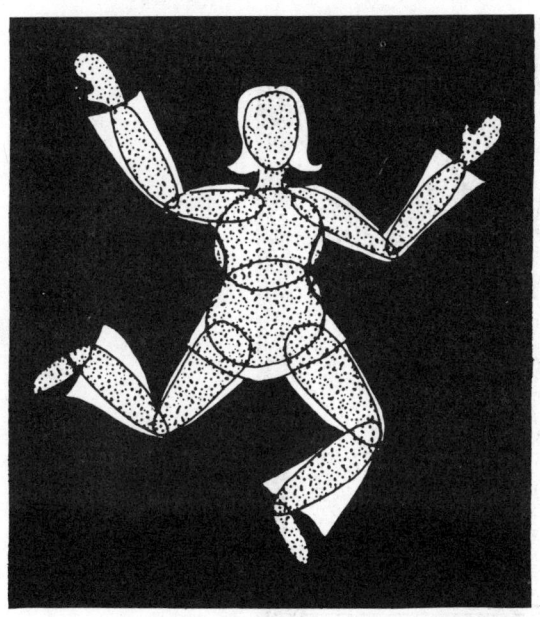

figure with a white crayon. After cutting out, the figures should be turned over to the "clean" side, so that the concept of the silhouettes is thoroughly grasped. Perhaps a "eureka" experience may occur here, and many students may want to create second or third figures if time permits. Final selection for display should be left to the students.

Display

Make two stacks of 12" × 18" paper in two shades of grey; include four sheets in each stack. Draw some simple tree trunks on the top sheet of each stack and then cut them out—four at a time.

In a similar stacking pattern, use seven sheets of 9" × 12" pink and seven sheets of 9" × 12" lavender, and from them cut out free-form clumps of foilage. (You won't be able to cut through seven thicknesses of paper at once, so it will be necessary to thin the stacks.)

Last of all you need ten orange hills and ten light green hills; these can be any size you choose to make them.

Begin to put up the display by taping two of the hills above your eye level. Put three or four more in a second row which slightly overlaps the first. Include more hills in each subsequent row, alternating colors and sizes as you progress.

Dynamic Figures

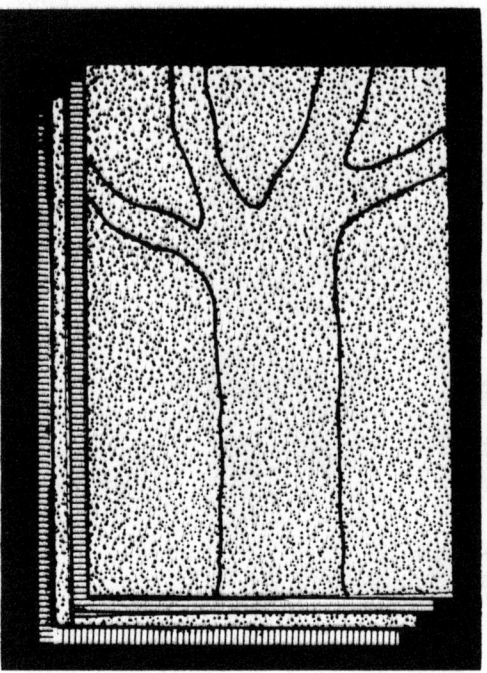

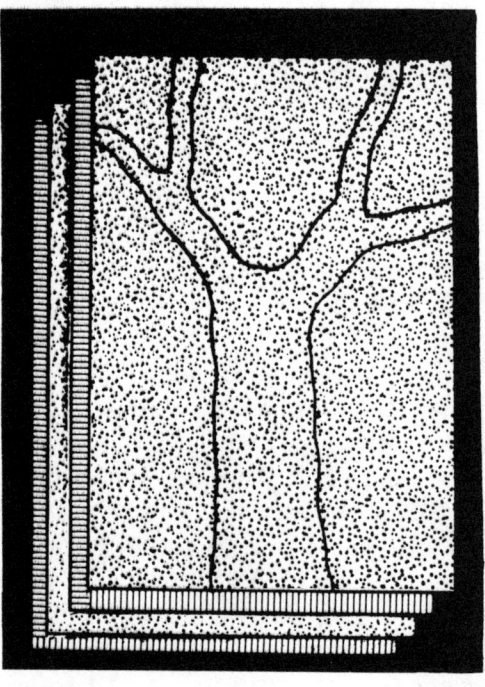

Dynamic Figures

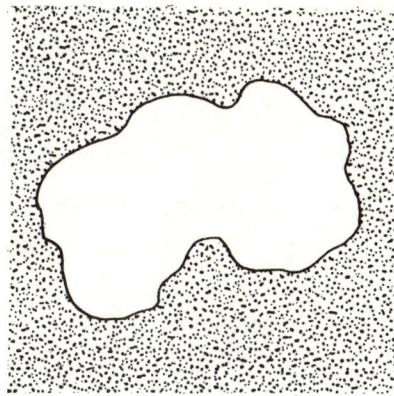 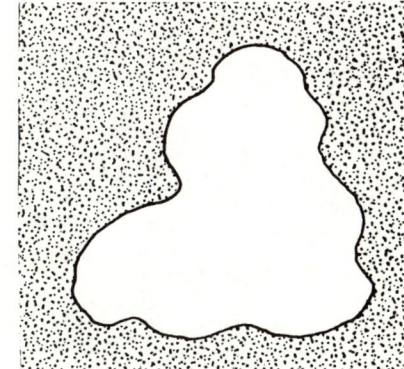

When the supply of hills has been exhausted, put up the trees. Work from background to foreground, and top off each tree with one or two clumps of foliage before putting up another. A great deal of overlapping of trees will be necessary to achieve the effect of distance and set the stage for the silhouettes.

Sort out the figures into five size categories. Begin to put them up by taping the smallest ones at the top of the display in grouped positions best suited to the activity; then work toward the foreground. The largest of the figures will end up at the bottom of the display and complete the overall depth effect.

The display tag might be a sign nailed to a tree announcing a marvelous picnic:

which becomes perpetual, since it will always be "today."

Dynamic Figures

Index

A

Alligators
   drawing, 51
   spring display, 50
Animal forms
   alligators, 51
   camel, 127
   cat, 24, 148
   chicken, 89, 159
   cow, 27
   donkey, 68
   fox, 157
   horse, 33
   kangaroo, 55
   lion, 111, 144
   mice, 61
   porcupine, 124
   rabbit, 120
Apiary, 80
April showers, 97, 179
Aviary enclosures, 37

B

Balloons, ascension, 188
Balloonist, 190
Bees, 81
Berry baskets, uses for
   ascension balloons, 188
   Easter baskets, 106
   fence, 31
   picture frames, 106
Birds
   chickens, 89, 159
   comical, 40, 176
   crows, 176
   decorative, 63
   partridges, 64
Birdcage, 38
Boat, 202
Boots, 179

Boxes
   as display vehicle, 85
   berry, 31, 105, 106, 188
   egg cartons, 113, 142, 143
   organizers for scrap paper, 7
Branches, as display units, 122
Bricks, simulated, printing of, 119
Broom straw, uses for
   lions, 145
   rabbits, 121
Buildings
   castle, 72
   city, 147
   farm, 87, 160
   henhouse, 88
   houses, 77
   tent, 130
Buttons, uses for
   buttons, 199
   decoration, 132
   eyes, 41

C

Cabbages, 56
Cages, bird, 37
Camels, 127
Carousel, 34
Carpet, padding, uses for
   alligators, 51
   hats, 175
Carpeting scraps, uses for
   beard, 100
   floor covering, 133
   fur, 111
   giant snake, 137
   hair, 198
   leaves, 130
   space craft, 85
Castle, 72
   bartizans, 74
   crenelated walls, 73
   turrets, 75

Caterpillars
    giant, group project, 140
    individual small, 139
Cats
    body, 25, 148
    construction paper, 148
    drawing, 24, 148
    face, 25, 148-149
    painted, 25
Ceiling, used as display space
    balloon race, 192
    bees, 82
    bird cages, 41
    fish, 22
    rainclouds, 97
    suspended pictures, 107
Cellophane
    clock faces, 60
    gluing of, 79
    pool, 166
    puddles, 178
    raindrops, 97, 178
    sun, 113
    sunglasses, 124, 169
    windowpanes, 79
Chains
    flat paper, 39, 40
    small paper link, 41
Chickens
    cut-paper, 159
    painted, 89
Christmas
    display, 63
    ornaments, 66
Circles used in drawings
    apple, 103
    bee, 82
    caterpillar, 139, 140
    clocks, 59
    daffodil, 52
    eyes, 41
    human figure, 195, 210
    umbrella, 45, 46
"Clair de Lune," Debussy, 152
Clams
    display for, 42
    fresh water, 43
    shell construction, 44
Clocks
    antique, 59
    decorative case construction, 60
    numeral spacing, 59

Clouds
    for emphasis, 151
    paper fringe, 117
    rain, 180
    spring, 200
    steel wool, 97
Color
    accented neutrals, 70
    classification of, 7
    harmonious combinations of, 173
    tempera, essential, 93
    warm, 183
Cone
    construction of, 132
    hat, 100
    tower tops, 75
Cows, drawing, 27
Crayon-resist process
    bee hive, 82
    cabbage leaves, 57
    tree trunk, 186
Creative writing motivators
    "Balloon Race," 187
    "Calm Clams," 42
    "Caterpillars & Co.," 136
    "Comical Birds," 36
    "Cone Creatures," 131
    imaginary sea voyage, 203
    "Life Aboard a U.F.O.," 83
    medieval castle, 72
    "Seahorses and Octopuses," 166
    "Silhouettes' Picnic," 209
Crows, 176
Curriculum coordination
    creative writing, (see "Creative writ-
        ing motivators")
    letter recognition, 28
    science, 43, 59, 187
    social studies, 72, 77, 187, 201
Cylinder
    castle construction, 73
    framing device, 133
    projection device in display, 47
    telescope, 100

D

Daffodils
    three-dimensional construction of, 52
    in displays, 50, 118
Dandelions, 69

Debussy, 152
Desert, 129
Design, as decoration of form
    balloons, 189
    birdcage, 38
    birds, 65
    cats, 149
    fish, 22
    leaves, 182
Donkey
    drawing, 68
    game, 68
Dragonflies, 117
Dromedary, 126

E

Easels, 94
Easter
    baskets, 106
    eggs, 90
Egg cartons, uses for
    palm tree trunk, 142
    telescoped tree trunk, 113
Egg shells, uses for
    chicken yard, 160
    clams, 43
    Easter, 90
    henhouse, 87
Elves
    large, 94
    small, 154, 183
Excelsior, uses for
    chicken yard, 160
    henhouse, 90
    nest, 65
Eye construction
    buttons used as, 41
    crayon colored, 144-145, 149
    cut-paper, 41, 139, 159
    drawing, 112
    life-savers used as, 41
    painted, 196

F

Fall displays
    "Dancing Skeletons," 205
    "Elves at Work," 181
    "Paintings on Real Leaves," 92
    "Sit-down People," 167

Fabric scraps, uses for
    clothing of figures, 132, 194, 198, 203
    interior decoration, simulated, 85, 132
    tents, 130
    turtles, 115
    umbrellas, 179
Feathers, uses for
    birds, 41, 65
    decorative accessories, 132, 198
    tree branches, 65
Fences
    brick, 119
    paper, 24, 170
    plastic, 31
    popsicle stick, 31
    semi 3-dimensional, 147
    stone, 198
    wire, 160
    wood-grained, 147
Fish
    drawing form, 19, 20
    seahorse, 164
    stuffed, 22
Flight, man's early means of, 188
Flowers
    daffodils, 52, 118
    dandelions, 69
    in raindrops, 97
Foil (package & gift-wrap remnants), uses for
    carousel, 34
    knights' armor, 75
    simulated jewelry, 132, 198
    wet rocks, 166
Foxes, 157
Framing of pictures
    berry baskets, 106, 107
    easel, 92
    hexagon, 80
    matt (simulated), 196
    raindrop, 96
    scalloped, 104
    star, 100
    window, 79

G

Geometric forms in displays
    hexagon, 81
    rectangle, 147
    star, 86, 99, 169

Geometric forms in drawings
    circle, 41, 45, 46, 52, 59, 82, 103, 139, 140, 195, 210
    oval, 27, 30, 40, 81, 84, 158, 194
    rectangle, 127
    triangle, 33, 43, 126, 127
Geometric shapes used in construction
    boxes, 85
    cones, 75, 100, 132
    cylinders, 47, 73, 100, 133
    hemispheres, 43
Gluing process
    cellophane, 79
    clamps for, 132
    time required with plastic, 120
Grandstand, three dimensional, 168

H

Hair
    carpet scrap, 100
    rope, 129
    string, 196
    yarn, 139
Hanger, paper clip
    Christmas ornament, 66
    hook, 22
    projecting, 134
"Happiness," A.A. Milne, 178
Hens, 159
Henhouse, 88
Hexagon, pattern for, 81
Hinges
    metal, 44
    paper, 82, 104
Hive, bee, magnified, 80
Horses
    carousel, 32
    drawing, 33
    sea, 161
Houses
    bird, 37, 88
    medieval, 72
    tent, 130
    Victorian, 77
Human body
    cut-paper, 194
    drawing, 169
    moving, 194, 210
    sitting, 167
    skeleton, 206-207
Humpty Dumpty, 197

I

Identity projection
    cone creatures, 131
    lift-up paintings, 102
    sit-down people, 167
    silhouettes, 209
    Victorian houses, 77
    walnut-head people, 193
Imaginary creatures
    elves, 151, 181
    extra-planetary, 85, 99
    Humpty Dumpties, 197
    three dimensional, 131
Insect forms
    bee, 80
    caterpillar, 136
    dragonfly, 117

K

Kangaroo, 55

L

Larva, (see Caterpillar)
Leaves
    cabbage, 56-57
    clusters in drawing, 29, 215
    coloring and decorating, 183
    dandelion, 69
    feather, 65, 113
    mounting for display, 94
    palm, 113, 130, 143
    pressed for painting, 93
    stylized drawings of, 182
    vine, 138 (illus.), 140
Lions
    sitting, 144
    standing, 111

M

Macintosh, 179
Medieval period, 34, 75, 100
Mice, 61
Milne, A.A., 178
Mollusks, 42
Moon, as display unit
    with cats, 25, 146
    with elves, 151

Moon, as display unit *(cont.)*
   with foxes, 156
Mushrooms, 152
Music as motivator, 152, 175

N

Newspaper as paper source, 143
Nighttime scenes
   "Alley Cats," 23
   "City Cats," 146
   "Little Foxes and Chickens," 156
Nursery rhymes
   "Hickory Dickory Dock," 62
   "Humpty Dumpty," 200
Nutshells, uses for
   heads, 194
   utensils, simulated, 85

O

Octopus, 162
Ovals used in drawings
   bee, 81
   bird, 40
   cow, 27
   fox, 158
   horse, 33
   people, 194
   space craft, 84

P

Palette, 94
Palm trees
   large, 143
   small, 113, 130
Partridge, 64
Patterns
   circle, 137
   cone, 132
   egg, 199
   hexagon, 81
   reasons for using, 99, 198
   pennies used as, 137
Perspective, point, modified use of, 191
Plastic packing material
   bubbles, 22
   clouds, 97
   porcupines, 123
   rabbits, 118

Plastic packing material *(cont.)*
   skeletons, 205
   source of, 206
   straw, 156, 160
   suction cups, 163
Poetry as motivator
   "Happiness," 178
   "Hickory Dickory Dock," 62
   "Humpty Dumpty," 200
Popsicle sticks, uses for
   fence, 31
   umbrella, 179
Porcupines, 124
Posts, mounting, 34

R

Rabbits, 120
Raincoat, 179
Raindrops, 95, 178
Rectangles used in drawings
   buildings, 147
   camels, 127
Reptiles
   alligator, 50
   snake, 136
   turtle, 114
"Rite of Spring," Stravinsky, 175
Rocks simulated for display, 166
Rodents
   mice, 58
   porcupine, 122
   rabbit, 118
Rope, uses for
   birds, 41
   camels' hair, 128
   human hair, 196
   snake, 137
   tails, 111

S

Sailors, 203
Sandpaper, uses for
   beach, 46
   dunes, 130
   sharpening scissors, 46
Scarecrow, 173
Scrap materials, utilization of
   bark, tree, 130
   beads, 85

Scrap materials, utilization of *(cont.)*
    berry baskets, 31, 105, 106, 188
    branches, 121
    broom straws, 121, 145
    buttons, 41, 132, 199
    carpeting scraps, 85, 100, 111, 130, 132, 137, 198
    carpet padding, 51, 175
    cellophane (wrapping from packages), 79, 178, 124, 169
    chicken wire, 87, 160
    cork, 130
    egg cartons, 113, 142
    eggshells, 43, 87, 90, 160
    excelsior, 65, 90, 160
    fabric scraps, 85, 115, 130, 175, 178, 194, 198, 203
    feathers, 41, 64, 132, 198
    foil (package and gift wrap), 34, 75, 132, 166, 198
    grass, dried, 175
    hose segment, garden, 137
    junk jewelry, 132
    leaves, pressed, 92
    newspaper, 143
    nutshells, 85, 194
    plastic bubbles, 22
    plastic packing pieces, 119, 160, 163, 206
    popsicle sticks, 31, 179
    rope, 41, 111, 128, 137, 196
    sandpaper, 46, 130
    seeds, 199
    spools, empty, 85
    straws, drinking, 76, 93
    styrofoam packing sheets, 97, 123
    twigs, 85, 200
    wallpaper, 79, 85, 198
    weeds, dried, 116, 125, 166, 199
    window shade, 119
Seahorses, 164
Shading with crayon, 29-31
Shelf displays, 133
Silhouettes
    buildings, 146, 160
    fox, 156, 160
    people, 209
Skeletons, 205
Snake, 138
Spacecraft, 84
Spectators, 167
Spring displays
    alligators and daffodils, 50

Spring displays *(cont.)*
    caterpillars and flowers, 136
    elves and mushrooms, 152
    Humpty Dumpties, 197
    rabbits and daffodils, 118
    raincoated figures and umbrellas, 177
    raindrops, 95, 97
    scarecrows, 173
Stairs, three dimensional, 168
Stars
    display decoration, 86
    for students' use, 169
    picture frame, 98
Steamship, 202
Steel wool, 97
Stravinsky, "Rite of Spring," 175
Straws, drinking, uses for
    flagpoles, 76
    paint brush holders, 93
Styrofoam sheets, uses for
    clouds, 97
    stem holder, 123
Summer scenes
    balloonists, 187
    camels in desert, 126
    caterpillars, 136
    cows in pasture, 26
    clams, ocean, beach and umbrellas, 42
    donkeys and dandelions, 67
    porcupines, 122
    sailors on shipdeck, 201
    silhouettes at picnic site, 209
Sun as display unit
    "Cabbages and Kangaroos," 57
    "Donkeys and Dandelions," 67
    "Lions and Palm Tree," 142
    "Porcupines," 122
    "Rope Camels," 126
    "Scarecrows," 172
    "Seahorses and Octopuses," 161
    "Shaggy Lions," 110
Swamp, 116
Symmetry in decorations, 38, 60

T

Telescope, 100
Telescoping
    cylinders, 100
    palm tree trunks, 113

Tempera paints
    essential colors, 93
    organized distribution, 93
Tentacles, octopus, 162, 163
Tents, 130
Texture
    bark, 143
    feathers, 40, 159
    flowers, 69
    fur, 111
    fuzz, 132, 139
    gills, mushroom, 153
    leaves, 31, 57
    quills, 122
    scales, 50, 51
    shells, 44
    sound, 111
    stones, 119, 73
    straw, 160, 175
Three-dimensional projects
    cabbages, 54
    clams, 42
    cone creatures, 131
    elf tree, 181
    "Life Aboard a U.F.O.," 83
    medieval castle, 72
    paintings in baskets, 105
    porcupines, 122
    shaggy lions, 110
    sitting people, 167
    stuffed paper fish, 18
Toothpicks, uses for
    pennant staffs, 169
    porcupine quills, 122
    U.F.O. interiors, 85
Trees
    bark, 130, 184
    branches, display, 121
    coloring, 29
    drawing, 28
    feather, 65
    giant, construction paper, 184-186
    palm, 113, 130, 143
Triangles used in drawings
    camels, 127
    chains, 41
    clam shells, 43
    horse's neck, 33
    sand dunes, 126
Turtles, 115
Twigs, uses for
    miniature plants, 85

Twigs, uses for *(cont.)*
    small tree branches, 200

U

Umbrellas
    beach, 45, 125
    carousel, 35
    rain, 179

V

Very easy projects
    "City Cats," 146
    "Fabric and Paper Turtles," 114
    "Giant Beehive," 80
    "Giant Caterpillar," 140
    "Humpty Dumpties," 197
    "Lions and Palm Trees," 142
    "Paintings in a Basket," 105
    "Pear in a Partridge Tree," 63
    "Raincoated Puddle-Jumpers," 177
    "Raindrops," 95
    "Shaggy Lions," 110
    "Silhouettes' Picnic," 209
    "Star Worlds," 98
    "Stuffed Paper Fish," 18
Vine, 140
Volleyball net as display unit, 19, 22
Voyage, imaginary, as motivator, 203

W

Walls
    brick, 119
    crenelated, 74
    stone, 198
Wallpaper, uses for
    collage, 198
    wall covering, 79, 85
Watercolors, 76
Water creatures
    alligators, 50
    clams, 42
    fish, 19
    octopuses, 162
    sailors, 202
    seahorses, 164
    turtles, 114
Water scenes
    "Alligators in Daffodil Land," 50

Water scenes *(cont.)*
   "Calm Clams," 42
   "Fabric and Paper Turtles," 114
   "Raincoated Puddle-Jumpers," 177
   "Raindrops," 95
   "Sailors on a Yacht," 201
   "Seahorses and Octopuses," 161
Wax-resist process, (see Crayon-resist)
Weeds, dried, uses for
   collage, 199
   display units, 116, 125, 166
Wings
   bee, 82

Wings *(cont.)*
   bird, 40, 176
   chicken, 89
Wizard, 100
Wood graining
   crayon, 147
   paint and crayon, 184

Y

Y, use of in drawing, 28
Yacht, 202